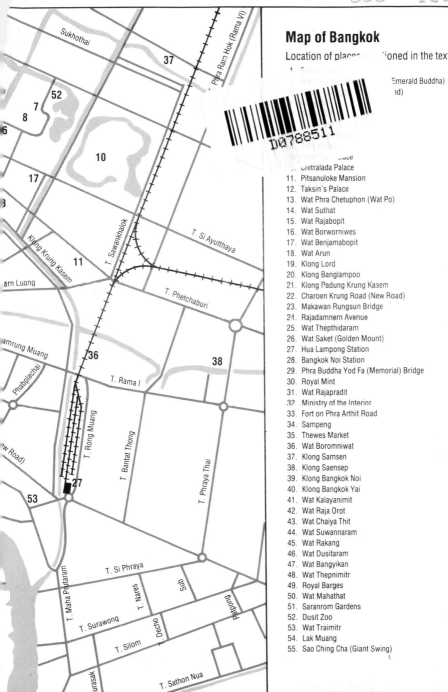

Map of Bangkok

Location of places mentioned in the text

Emerald Buddha)
d)

...ace
9. Chitralada Palace
11. Pitsanuloke Mansion
12. Taksin's Palace
13. Wat Phra Chetuphon (Wat Po)
14. Wat Suthat
15. Wat Rajabopit
16. Wat Borworniwes
17. Wat Benjamabopit
18. Wat Arun
19. Klong Lord
20. Klong Banglampoo
21. Klong Padung Krung Kasem
22. Charoen Krung Road (New Road)
23. Makawan Rungsun Bridge
24. Rajadamnern Avenue
25. Wat Thepthidaram
26. Wat Saket (Golden Mount)
27. Hua Lampong Station
28. Bangkok Noi Station
29. Phra Buddha Yod Fa (Memorial) Bridge
30. Royal Mint
31. Wat Rajapradit
32. Ministry of the Interior
33. Fort on Phra Arthit Road
34. Sampeng
35. Thewes Market
36. Wat Boromniwat
37. Klong Samsen
38. Klong Saensep
39. Klong Bangkok Noi
40. Klong Bangkok Yai
41. Wat Kalayanimit
42. Wat Raja Orot
43. Wat Chaiya Thit
44. Wat Suwannaram
45. Wat Rakang
46. Wat Dusitaram
47. Wat Bangyikan
48. Wat Thepnimitr
49. Royal Barges
50. Wat Mahathat
51. Saranrom Gardens
52. Dusit Zoo
53. Wat Traimitr
54. Lak Muang
55. Sao Ching Cha (Giant Swing)

IMAGES OF ASIA
General Editor: MICHAEL SMITHIES

Old Bangkok

Other titles in the series

At the Chinese Table
T. C. LAI

Balinese Paintings
A. A. M. DJELANTIK

Chinese Jade
JOAN HARTMAN-GOLDSMITH

A Garden of Eden: Plant Life in South-East Asia
WENDY VEEVERS-CARTER

The Kris: Mystic Weapon of the Malay World
EDWARD FREY

Indonesian Batik: Processes, Patterns and Places
SYLVIA FRASER-LU

Macau
CESAR GUILLEN-NUÑEZ

Sailing Craft of Indonesia
ADRIAN HORRIDGE

Old Bangkok

MICHAEL SMITHIES

'*Krung Tep* they call this place of contradictions'
(H. W. Smyth, *Five Years in Siam*, 1898)

SINGAPORE
OXFORD UNIVERSITY PRESS
OXFORD NEW YORK
1986

Oxford University Press

Oxford New York Toronto
Petaling Jaya Singapore Hong Kong Tokyo
Delhi Bombay Calcutta Madras Karachi
Nairobi Dar es Salaam Cape Town
Melbourne Auckland

and associates in
Beirut Berlin Ibadan Nicosia

OXFORD is a trademark of Oxford University Press

© *Oxford University Press Pte. Ltd. 1986*

ISBN 0 19 582686 8

Printed in Singapore by Koon Wah Printing Pte. Ltd.
Published by Oxford University Press Pte. Ltd.,
Unit 221, Ubi Avenue 4, Singapore 1440

Contents

1 The Foundation of Bangkok   1

2 The Royal Palaces   7

3 The Major Temples   25

4 The Growth of Bangkok   35

5 Traditional Survivals   54

6 Oases in the New Bangkok   67

   Epilogue   76

   Appendix   78

   Glossary   80

   Bibliography   81

The Foundation of Bangkok

WHEN Ayutthaya fell to the Burmese in 1767, Siam was left without a king, a court or a capital. The siege had lasted for more than a year, and towards the end a number of persons, seeing the situation hopeless, discreetly withdrew from the city, including the Phya Tak, the lord of the town of Tak, who had been blamed for the failure of a counter-attack against the Burmese in 1766. Borommaracha, also known as Suriyamin, the last king of the dynasty (which had had several breaks in succession), was killed in the attack, as were many of his relatives; some who survived, including his brother Uchamphon, who had reigned for ten days in 1758, were taken captive by the triumphant Burmese. Ayutthaya was delivered up to the Burmese soldiers in an orgy of looting, rape and pillage; temples were destroyed and burnt, treasures seized and the capital, which had so impressed early European travellers, was demolished.

Though the destruction was great, the capital could have been re-established on the site it had occupied for over 400 years; a considerable quantity of building materials was later to be used in the construction of Bangkok, being brought down the river by barges. There were strategic considerations requiring a new site; Ayutthaya had been attacked and occupied by the Burmese twice in its history and was therefore too close for comfort to Siam's traditional enemy. The capital had to be re-established on a safer site, further from the Burmese. It also had to be established at a greater distance from Pitsanuloke, where one of the rival claimants to the throne had established himself. The capital, therefore, had to be nearer the sea.

It was Taksin, the Lord of Tak, who was to pull the kingdom

together again. It had split into five parts in 1767. In Fang, in the north, there was a group of power-mad red-clothed monks. In Pitsanuloke, to the north of Ayutthaya, there was a local governor who had himself crowned king. In the north-east, at Phimai near Khorat, Prince Thepphipit, a brother of the last Ayutthayan king, held sway. In Nakorn Srithammaraj, in the south, there was also a governor contesting the succession, but with the added claim to be an hereditary viceroy. Taksin had his own power base in Chantaburi to the south-east. By a series of campaigns, Taksin achieved by 1770 what had seemed three years previously impossible: he had re-established the whole kingdom and was its crowned king.

This achievement is often underestimated, if only because his reign was brief and was overshadowed by delusions towards its end. Taksin, an outsider with a Chinese father, took himself too seriously and his achievements went literally to his head; he required monks to recognize him as a form of deity and sought to fly through the air. A revolt in 1781 was led by Phraya Sankhaburi, a military commander in Thonburi. King Taksin abdicated and took monk's robes. His principal general, Phraya Chakri, was recalled from a campaign in Cambodia and invited in 1782 to accept the throne by rebels who had taken Thonburi. Phraya Chakri, subsequently known as Rama I, was well-connected with the influential families of Ayutthaya, but was away from the city at the time of its fall, in the service of the governor of Rajburi.

Taksin became a prisoner of King Rama I; an assembly of counsellors demanded the death penalty to which the new king agreed. Taksin asked for an audience with his royal successor, but Rama I refused his request 'with tears running down his face', according to the chronicles. In the presence of the king, Taksin was put to death according to the prescribed way of disposing of those descended of royal blood, by being tied in a velvet sack and beaten by a sandlewood club. Of his heir-

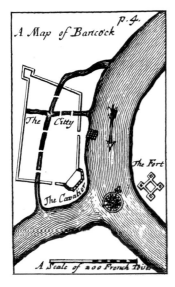

1. Map of Bancok (Loubère, 1693)

presumptive, who like his wife and sons had been imprisoned, tortured and flogged by the mad king, nothing is heard. Taksin had been too busy pulling the country together in the early years, and too concerned with religious prerogatives in the later ones, to be concerned about founding a dynasty. His body was burned in 1784, in a cremation sponsored by Rama I.

The formal proclamation of Rama I (Colour Plate 1) and his provisional coronation, including a procession on the Chao Phraya River, took place on 10 June 1782, and the king's younger brother was made the Maha Uparaj, sometimes known as Uparaj or 'Second King'. The Thiphakorawong Chronicle of 1869 laconically notes: 'The king first quelled the disorders on Thonburi, after which he came to decide that the east bank of the river was actually a better location than the west bank.'

Taksin had founded his capital at Thonburi, in what was known to Westerners in the seventeenth century, according to

3

their maps (Plate 1), as Bancok, the village of the wild plum, sometimes translated as a bitter olive ('ban' means village in Thai, and 'makok' or 'kok' the name of the tree). This was already well-defended in the middle of the seventeenth century. In fact, the main flow of the Chao Phraya River used to go behind it, following what are now known as Klong Bangkok Yai and Klong Bangkok Noi. A short canal or klong had been cut in the reign of King Prajai (1534–46) to eliminate several bends in the river and reduce the distance to Ayutthaya, but this canal soon became the main channel of the river, so that Bancok, now known as Thonburi, faced the river to the east, and the protruding bank opposite. The importance of the strategic site of this bank on the other side of the river had already been appreciated, and it seems that an Italian Jesuit with the French mission in the 1660s had built the first fort there. French engineers in 1675 reconstructed the forts on both banks and they were modernized by Chevalier de Forbin in 1686. But the French were forced to retreat ignominiously from their positions in 1688. It was to this site, the new fort at Bangkok, that Rama I moved his capital in 1782.

He did not do this so much as to set his own stamp on the land, but practical considerations were probably foremost. The site had already been recognized as more easily defensible than the west bank, and a month before Rama I became king, King Bodawpaya had seized the throne in Burma. Rama I rightly anticipated trouble from this traditional source.

Sternstein has examined the evidence and argues persuasively in favour of the notion that Taksin had all along intended to transfer his capital to the east bank, citing in particular the temporary nature of the structures in Thonburi and the initiation of the construction of the canal, Klong Lord, at the back of what was to become the palace area. Whatever the truth, which at this stage is unlikely to be known for certain, the site of the palace on the east bank was already occupied by Chinese

2. View of the City of Bangkok (Crawfurd, 1828)

merchants who included a number of rich persons. They had to be invited to remove themselves to a location beyond the walls of the new palace, and left to establish their community at what is now the Chinese quarter of Sampeng.

Although to country Thais Bangkok is still referred to as Bangkok, which is the name foreigners have always used, it assumed much grander names when it became the capital. At Rama I's coronation in 1782, he renamed the capital, using forty-three syllables for its title, starting Krung Thep Pra Maha Nakorn, 'the city of angels, the capital city...'. The official name was made even longer in 1786, though the beginning was virtually unchanged, and Krung Thep Maha Nakorn is now the name used to describe Greater Bangkok, incorporating the former capital and province of Thonburi as well. Both names given by Rama I incorporated the name of Ayutthaya (itself referring back to Ayodhya of the *Ramayana*) and he consciously set about creating a new capital worthy of the former great city which seventeenth-century visitors had found as large and wealthy as many cities in Europe at the time.

John Crawfurd, in his account of his abortive embassy to the court of Siam, left one of the earliest impressions (Plate 2) of Bangkok only forty years after its foundation.

March 29, 1822

The morning presented to us a very novel spectacle—the capital of Siam, situated on both sides of the Menam. Numerous temples of Buddha, with tall spires attached to them, frequently glittering with gilding, were conspicuous among the mean huts and hovels of the natives, throughout which were interspersed a profusion of palms, ordinary fruit-trees, and the sacred fig (*ficus religiosa*). On each side of the river there was a row of floating habitations, resting on rafts of bamboos, moored to the shore. These appeared the neatest and best description of dwellings; they were occupied by good Chinese shops. Close to these aquatic habitations were anchored the largest description of native vessels, among which were many junks of great size, just arrived from China. The face of the river presented a busy scene, from the number of boats and canoes of every size and description which were passing to and fro. The number struck us as very great at the time, for we were not aware that there are few or no roads at Bang-kok, and that the river and canals form the common highways, not only for goods, but for passengers of every description.

As he got to know the city better and visited its buildings hidden in the foliage, he modified his opinion of its architectural offerings, but the first impression, of busy animation and a verdant watery city, remained one that was accurate of Bangkok until very recent times.

2

The Royal Palaces

RAMA I'S palace was, as we have seen, constructed approximately on the site of the old French-built fort on the Bangkok side of the river, facing what was effectively now the temporary capital in Thonburi, and next to the old temple of Wat Potaram, which the king later enlarged and which is now generally known to Thais as Wat Phra Chetuphon (though foreigners obstinately cling to the contraction of the old name, Wat Po). Klong Lord was already built, and provided a strategic defence line to the east, beyond which stretched marshland subject, then and now, to periodic flooding.

The palace was, at first, the city, the seat of power, which had to look to its defences. These were not strong in the first instance; the chronicles note: '. . . [after the relocation of a group of Chinese people], the buildings for the royal residence were constructed and the whole compound was fenced in with temporary wooden walls so that the king could move in for the time being.' The high crenellated brick wall came later, and enclosed more than a square mile of land, according to Seidenfaden. The palace was built to be self-sufficient; the king need never leave his palace, and could show himself from a specially constructed balcony which still exists, overlooking the Saranrom Gardens next to the Ministry of Foreign Affairs. The palace contained an inner area, the wang nai, which was the women's quarters, effectively the royal harem, in which the only male permitted was the king himself.

The foundation of the palace was built on piles and the layout was planned to correspond precisely to the old palace in Ayutthaya. The palace of the Maha Uparaj, the Wang Na, sometimes known as the Palace of the Front, was begun at the same time and both were officially opened two months after the beginning of the construction work, which had, of course, started at an auspicious time determined by the court astrologers. The chronicles note that construction work continued for several years and as soon as the wooden buildings were habitable, bricks were obtained from Ayutthaya for use with more permanent buildings; even the fortifications of Thonburi were destroyed to provide building materials for the palace.

An early American visitor, Roberts, noted in 1837:

The most conspicuous objects which strike the eye of the traveller on the Menam, besides the splendid wats, are the new palace, a large watch-tower, and a prachade or tall thin spire, which is many feet higher than any other building; all are situated within the walls of the city. The palace itself, with its pagodas, and many other buildings, is surrounded by a high wall, having strong gates, and a guard of miserable and undisciplined militia. The palace is a handsome and extensive building of brick, and stuccoed; the doors and windows are similar in style, taste and outward decorations to the better class of temples, and bear a strong resemblance to the Gothic style of architecture.

Roberts' concept of Gothic, then relatively little known in the United States, is perhaps a trifle vague.

The palace was, of course, continually added to by different monarchs, and its appearance today is very different from that in Rama I's time. So too are its surroundings; the walls to the east faced directly on to the river, without a road intervening (Colour Plate 2). It was near here, at Ta Phra where subsequently the Wang Ta Phra (which became Silapakorn University) was built, that the statue of Phra Buddha Chakyamuni was landed after being brought from Sukhothai, for installation in Wat Suthat, which Rama I also started.

Two buildings which can be visited survive from Rama I's reign, the Amarin Winichai Hall (as it is usually known) and the Dusit Maha Prasat Throne Hall. The first (Plate 3) was built as

8

3. Hall of Audience, Palace of Bangkok (Mouhot, 1864)

an audience hall and is shaped like the letter T, with painted walls and ceiling; the throne was screened from visitors by heavy curtains that were drawn aside to reveal the royal presence, before which all prostrated themselves. The chronicles note:

A royal *prasat* audience hall was constructed within the palace grounds and was, on the king's personal order, done in the style of the Sanphetprasat Hall at the old capital of Ayutthaya. It was flanked on both sides by smaller buildings. The construction was completed and the roof spire finally put in place on Friday, the tenth day of the waxing moon of the fourth month, the Year of the Great Snake, the sixth year of the decade, the year 1146 of the Chula Era [1784].

A more elaborate coronation was held in 1785 and the king carefully followed 'the formulas practiced in traditional times'. By doing so, the king is stated to have felt that 'this would bring good fortune to himself, good fortune in governmental affairs and thus happiness to all the people of the kingdom'. At the same time his son was granted 'the palace of the late King of Thonburi'.

However, in 1798 lightning struck the Amarind Winichai Hall and it caught fire. Everyone from the royal family went to help put it out: 'The king ordered government officials to get together and carry out the pearl-decorated throne under the royal tiered umbrella inside the audience hall. This was done in time to save it from the fire.' The king was of course extremely worried about the omens of such an event, and had Pali texts searched to discover what meaning might be attributed to this calamity. The monks wisely found no obstacle to continuing progress of the dynasty, and a new hall was ordered to be built, slightly smaller than the previous one. However, it was covered in tin, like the old building, so it was just as likely to be struck by lightning again.

The other building dating from the time of Rama I is the Dusit Maha Prasat Throne Hall which was built in 1789 (Plate 4). It is shaped like a cross with arms of equal length, has painted walls and lacquered and gilded doors and windows. The throne is in the centre of the hall. The roofline is topped by a gilded spire. This relatively simple building, with its painted walls, is used for special ceremonies and for lying-in-state.

It was the Amarin Winichai Hall that Crawfurd described when delivering his embassy in 1822:

The throne and its appendages occupied the whole of the upper end of the hall. The first was gilded all over, and about fifteen feet high. It has much the shape and look of a handsome pulpit. A pair of curtains, of gold tissue upon a yellow ground, concealed the whole of the upper part of the room, except the throne; and they were intended to be drawn over this also, except when used. In front of the throne, and rising from the floor, were to be seen a number of gilded umbrellas of various sizes .... The King, as he appeared seated on his throne, had more the appearance of a statue in a niche than of a living being. He wore a loose gown of gold tissue, with very wide sleeves. His head was

4. Dusit Maha Prasat (Mouhot, 1864)

bare, for he wore neither crown nor any other ornament on it. Close to him was a golden baton or sceptre....

It is in this hall that today the king sometimes receives the credentials of foreign envoys, though with less pomp than described by Crawfurd.

The main buildings of the palace in which state functions were held, Dusit Maha Prasat, Amarin Winichai, Chakrapat Phiman and Phaisan Thaksin, were all extensively repaired in the reign of Rama III and all four were given new roofs.

The principal building in the palace to be found today was completed in 1882. It replaced an earlier building in which the Montigny embassy from France was received (Plate 5). Located between the two surviving examples of Rama I's palace, which are splendid examples of traditional Siamese architecture, it presents an agreeable mixture of Eastern and Western styles (Plate 6). The building proper is in the Italian Renaissance style, with a central balcony and a double approach stairway, while

5. French ambassadors at the Grand Palace, the Montigny embassy during the reign of Rama IV

the roof (the plan of the British architect John Chinitz was actually changed during the construction) is a Siamese tiered structure with three spires of a seven-tier mondop or receding square style. The rooms are decorated in the heavy late nineteenth-century European style and the ashes of deceased monarchs are kept on the topmost level. State banquets are held in the banqueting hall and there is an elaborate audience hall. The Chakri Throne Hall to be found here is also sometimes used when ambassadors present their credentials.

The courtyards of the palace seem endless, and one leads into another with ease, each with well-kept lawns and decorative clipped trees. One of the most charming, Suan Sivalai, is around the marble chapel of Buddha Ratanasathan, built by Rama IV, behind the modern Boromphiman Palace where state visitors stay and which was used for a short period by Crown Prince Vachiravudh and also Kings Ananda Mahidol and Bhumibol; the courtyard on the evening of the king's birthday used to

6. Leaving the Chief Palace in Bangkok (Birdwood, 1900)

present a glittering scene at which 'le tout Bangkok' was present. It should be pointed out that several buildings in the outer palace are at present occupied by government departments, notably the Ministry of Finance, which is due to move before long.

7. Luang Mae Cha (Khian), head of the female guardians in the Grand Palace and for a time the head of the women's police of 'The Inside'

The Inside, the women's quarters, was quite special. There was a special Directress of the Inside with her own police force (Plate 7), the *krom klone*, who were drilled like soldiers. The population was huge, as each queen had her own substantial retinue of more than 200 attendants, some of which had their own servants and each minor wife had a large number of people to serve and help her (Plate 8). The area was congested and without sanitation, with water being carried away in pails. Malcolm Smith, who was the physician to Queen Saovapha, who was raised in the Inner Palace, writes:

8. Consorts, sisters and daughters of H.M. King Chulalongkorn. The large
   family of King Chulalongkorn adopted a modified form of Western
   dress as part of the modernization programme.

The harem was a town complete in itself, a congested network of
houses and narrow streets, with gardens, lawns, artificial lakes and
shops. It had its own government, its own institutions, its own laws
and law-courts. It was a town of women, controlled by women. Men
on special work of construction or repair were admitted, and the
doctors when they came to visit the sick. The King's sons could live
there until they reached the age of puberty . . . . But the only man who
lived within its walls was the King.

Of course, there was a great deal of speculation about what
went on in the Inner Palace, but few incidents of intruders have
come down. One is authenticated by the Thiphakarawong
Chronicle, written in the fifth reign, though referring back to
events under Rama III. In 1838, says Vella, a young official
pursued his suit for one of the royal concubines:

The couple had never met or spoken face to face, but they had,
through go-betweens, exchanged gifts, poems and professions of love.
The couple agreed that the concubine must seek a release from the

king's harem and one of the palace officials had been approached for aid when the entire affair was disclosed to the king by one of the go-betweens. The king turned the matter over to a jury for a decision. The jury concluded that, according to the laws, professions of love between any man and a woman of the harem constituted an offense calling for the death penalty, and that any person who aided the couple or knew of the affair and did not report it should be subject to the same punishments. As a result of this decision, ten persons were executed; the principals, the palace official, the go-betweens (with the exception of the one who reported the affair), two brothers of the young official who knew of the affair and three soothsayers who had told the young official he would get his wishes.

There was, in fact, a similar incident recorded of a love affair between an Ai Khian and one of King Mongkut's commoner-wives, Chom Chau Choi. The judges decided that Ai Khian and his wife Ai Kularb, who rather strangely had acted as go-between, should, in the words of the chronicles, 'be put to death at the Makasan Temple on Tuesday, the twelfth day of the waxing moon in the seventh month [1859]'.

The atmosphere of the Inner Court is powerfully captured by Kukrit Pramoj in his popular contemporary novel, *Four Reigns*. His heroine is brought up in the palace, a society with which the author was intimately acquainted. He notes:

...the Inner Court with its highways and byways was still a vast territory to her and never lacking in adventure. She made visits and discoveries. She went everywhere, or virtually everywhere.... She had been to the Yellow Room. Lying as it did directly in the path between His Majesty's Private Apartments and the Front Chambers where he conferred with his Ministers, this was where the ladies of the Inner Court foregathered to pay their respects as he walked by....

The Temple of the Emerald Buddha, Wat Phra Keo, is the royal chapel and is part of the palace complex. It too was built by Rama I, in conscious imitation of the royal chapel in Ayutthaya, Wat Sri Sanphet. Rama I, as King Taksin's general, had conquered Vientaine and brought the famed statue of the emerald Buddha, which is in fact made of a kind of jasper, to the capital, where it was kept at Wat Arun in Thonburi until being transferred to its present shrine in 1784. The chronicles note that the image was 'transported from its temporary shelter at the former Palace on the west bank. The statue was put on a gilt royal barge, followed by a procession of other boats and taken across the river to the newly constructed temple'.

The temple has been much described and is rightly considered one of the most impressive and extraordinary complexes anywhere. The courtyards are a riot of colour and lavish buildings, and the confined space, particularly when packed with worshippers, enhances one's memory of the scene. The main sanctuary, which was brilliantly restored in 1982 for the 200th anniversary of the founding of Bangkok, is raised on a marble platform and the walls have gilded garudas going all around the base. Three pairs of inlaid mother-of-pearl doors lead inside, where the altar, crowned by the relatively small statue clothed in gold, dominates. The fresco paintings date from the second quarter of the nineteenth century and that behind the doors shows the struggle of the Buddha against the spirit of Mara.

Most of the other buildings in the temple complex were added later. The paintings of the cloister have been restored many times. To the right of the temple is a group of structures on an east–west axis. Closest to the entrance is the Prasat Phra Thepbidon, or royal pavilion, a very ornate building in the shape of a cross, originally dating from 1855 but much modified after a fire in 1903; it is only opened once a year when the Chakri dynasty is celebrated. Behind it is the mondop, or library, with a stepped Thai-style roof supported on gilded square columns. This was built by Rama I to house the first revised Buddhist scriptural canon which he had commissioned. Behind this is a gilded chedi, or tapering spire, Phra Si Ratana

Chedi, in the Singalese style, built by Rama IV in 1855 and containing a relic of the Buddha. Near by is a model of Angkor Wat, also ordered by Rama IV but completed by his successor: from 1769, when Taksin annexed the provinces of Siam Reap and Battambang, until 1907, when the provinces were ceded to France by treaty, Angkor was in the territory of the Thai kings.

The Temple of the Emerald Buddha is not a large complex, and it is less the scale than the decorative profusion of spires, prang (Cambodian-style square spires), guardian giants, kinaree (mythical birds) and other statues, as well as the brilliant colours and glitter of gold which strike the visitor. Viewed from outside the palace walls, from the Pramane Ground, called in Thai Sanam Luang, the plain white wall contrasts exquisitely with the profusion of gilded roofs and spires that comprise the palace and its sacred temple.

The Sanam Luang, meaning 'royal ground', is the scene of the elaborate royal cremations, and on this account used to be known in Thai as Thung Pramen, which is the name foreigners have kept. Across from this is what remains of the Palace of the 'Second King', the Wang Na. To avoid confusion, Rama IV used to sign himself, when writing in English, 'the Supreme King of Siam'. The institution of the second king confused Westerners a great deal and the position of second king (Uparaj) was allowed to lapse in Rama V's reign, when the palace buildings were given over for use as a museum, which they remain. The second king was a kind of reserve monarch, usually a brother of the reigning king, who had all the trappings of kingship, including his own troops, but not the ultimate power. There is no instance of a second king appointed by the supreme king on his accession succeeding to the throne in the Bangkok period, but that may be as much an accident of human mortality as design. However, Rama I's brother in this position died and the supreme king appointed a second Second King, his son, who became Rama II.

The buildings that survive from the old palace were also

originally constructed in 1782. The principal structure is the elegant temple Wat Buddhaisawan, facing the Sanam Luang, with wall paintings which have been carefully restored. The present chapel dates from 1787 and the paintings from shortly afterwards. They show twenty-eight scenes from the life of the Buddha, with four ranks of heavenly worshippers above. There are fine details of figures and foliage set in a natural background. The Buddha statue, which is known as Phra Buddha Sihing, is of bronze and dates from the Sukhothai period. At the rear of the temple, on the inside, are several huge gilded and lacquered bookcases of the late Ayutthaya and early Bangkok periods.

Behind Wat Buddhaisawan is what remains of the old palace structure proper. It is a very extensive building, with a square-columned throne hall at the front which was added in the third reign. Behind this is the original complex of eleven inter-connected buildings, some raised in height, and small court-yards. With whitewashed walls and coffered ceilings, these structures have a great deal of charm.

They contain musical instruments, dance objects, some porcelain, old typewriters, arms, some textiles, litters and a caprisoned elephant belonging to the collection of the National Museum, which is mostly housed in the two ugly modern buildings which dwarf the old palace on both of its sides. This is not the place to describe the museum collection, but mention should be made of the Tamnak Deng, to the left of Wat Buddhaisawan, a teak dwelling that was originally the residence of an elder sister of Rama I. It was moved from the palace to Thonburi for the consort of Rama II, Queen Sri Suriyen, one of whose sons was Pin Klao, the second king of Rama IV. Pin Klao had the house, in which he had once lived, moved to his palace compound. It is quite simple and with a verandah in front; inside is an excellent collection of elaborate furniture of the early Bangkok period, some of the objects having belonged to Queen Sri Suriyen.

At the rear of the National Museum complex and outside its

grounds, is a small temple commonly known as Wat Phra Keo Wang Na. It was built by the second king in the reign of Rama III and is now in the grounds of the College of Theatrical Arts. The building is square in plan, with protruding sections, and is without inside columns. The paintings, dating from Rama IV, are extremely interesting and tell the story of the Phra Buddha Sihing image (Rama IV considered at one time moving the image to this temple).

King Chulalongkorn, Rama V, was oppressed by the stuffiness of the overcrowded Grand Palace and to escape from it used to go with his family on trips out of Bangkok. After his European tour of 1897, and impressed with royal residences outside city centres, he acquired land between Klong Padung Krung Kasem and Klong Samsen to inaugurate in 1899 Suan Dusit ('Celestial Garden'). This was at the end of the avenue conceived as the Siamese Champs Elysées, along which the king and younger members of his family and the court would cycle for exercise and fresh air when official duties at the Grand Palace permitted.

In 1901 the king ordered the dismantling of a huge teak palace, started in 1893, on Koh Sri Chang, an island beyond Chonburi to the south-east. The building was reconstructed, with Prince Naris (Narisaranuwatiwong) as architect, at Vimanmek (Colour Plate 3), to which the king and court removed. He lived there from 1901-7, when he moved into a European-style palace in Suan Dusit, Ambharasathan. The wooden palace was little used after 1907 and not at all after 1925. The glories of the building were rediscovered by Queen Sirikit who had it restored and it was opened to the public in 1985. It is a remarkable building both for its size and contents and for its setting in magnificent grounds.

Vimanmek Palace (Plate 9) is an L-shaped building, stucco and brick on the ground floor, with two main floors in teak above, and the topmost private quarters in the octagon on the

9. Princes waiting for H.M. King Chulalongkorn, taken in Vimanmek Palace

fourth floor. It contains thirty-one suites of rooms, all decorated in the turn-of-the-century biedermeier style, with European, Siamese, Chinese and even Russian *objets d'art*. The throne room, the king's study, his private bathroom, the banqueting hall, the music room with its period piano, and the royal insignia, are all on display. There are two impressive surrounding buildings: the Apisek Dusit Throne Hall, a single-storey fretwork gingerbread teak construction with what appears to be some Indian decorative inspiration, and Ruen Ton, a group of Thai-style buildings for visitors and guests, built beside a large pool in the palace grounds.

King Chulalongkorn commissioned the huge marble throne hall which stands at the end of Rajadamnern Avenue, in the centre of the Dusit area. It was consciously designed by the king to be a focal point at the end of the royal street and also to be an indicator of the international modernity of his realm. Italian architects produced an imposing classical building topped by a cupola, which is decorated on the inside, like the other domes forming the ceiling, with paintings showing episodes in Thai history, more particularly of the Chakri dynasty. The engineers of the time had some trouble with the foundations of so heavy a building in the soft Bangkok soil. The hall was completed after the death of Rama V but was only used for a few years as it was intended, before becoming the seat of the legislature after the overthrow of the absolute monarchy. A new legislative assembly has now been built beyond Vimanmek Palace; the Throne Hall facing Rajadamnern is not normally open to the public.

The Dusit area remained popular. Some of Rama V's numerous retinue were accommodated in small houses which later became part of Suan Sunantha Teacher Training College. He started a little to the east of Dusit on Rajavithi Road the Phya Thai Palace for carrying out agricultural experiments in the grounds. His First Queen from 1895, Saovapha, and the mother of the sixth and seventh kings, died there in 1919. Her physician records a marvellous detail about her habits. She kept the same noctural hours as her late husband, going to bed at six in the morning: 'Nothing was allowed to disturb [the palace's] tranquillity. All traffic on the road outside was diverted.... Not even the birds were allowed to intrude, and to keep them away two men armed with blow-pipes and clay bullets—noiseless weapons—and accompanied by an old woman, ceaselessly patrolled the grounds.' Her son, Vachiravudh, after her death pulled down most of the buildings except the throne hall and had them rebuilt, staying there from 1922 to 1925 when he died. The palace then became a hotel under the operation of the Royal State Railways, after that a radio station, and since 1946 has been part of Phra Mongkut Klao Military Hospital.

It was Rama VI who built a villa in the Dusit area and renamed it Chitralada, which is the residence of the present monarch. Rama VI was a great builder, and dotted Bangkok with residences built for various members of the court, though they were not royal palaces. An example is Pitsanuloke Mansion, the present official residence of the prime minister, the house built by the king for Phraya Aniruttheva, a commoner, in an elaborate Venetian baroque style.

Bangkok was, however, full of palaces, for the royal progeny of King Chulalongkorn was numerous. The present Ministry of Education, Wang Chandrakasem, was built by Rama V for Vachiravudh when crown prince, but it was never occupied by him, since Rama V died before it was completed. This was similar to the fate of Wang Saranrom, now the Ministry of Foreign Affairs, which was built in 1866 at the end of the reign of Rama IV for Chulalongkorn when crown prince, but King Mongkut died before his heir could live there. Instead, a younger brother took up residence in the palace. Rama VI as crown prince stayed here from 1902 until 1910, when the building was given to its present occupants for its work and for entertaining government guests.

Among the many other palaces which have assumed a modern functional use, like the Ministry of Education and Ministry of Foreign Affairs, and like them are now dominated by less gracious modern structures, is the former home of the Prince of Nakorn Sawan in the grounds of the Bank of Thailand by the river. Wang Ta Phra, by the Grand Palace, is an amalgamation of three palaces, one of which was built for a nephew of Rama I. The buildings were rebuilt by Rama V and were recently given to Silapakorn University. However, another royal palace which is still in use is Patumwan Palace, at present occupied by the Princess Mother.

The old palace of King Taksin still exists in Thonburi, next to Wat Arun and at the end of the appropriately named Tanon Prarachawang Derm (Road of the Old Palace). Since 1907 it has been used by the Thai navy; previously it had been occupied by a number of royal princes, the first being Prince Israsundorn, son of Rama I, who succeeded him to the throne. The throne hall, the shrine of King Taksin, three Chinese-style mansions and the Wichaiprasit Fort, dating from the seventeenth century, survive. The palace was occupied by Taksin from 1771 to 1782, but was abandoned for a time after Rama II came to the throne in 1809. Thirteen years later Crawfurd would write: 'Farther up the river, on its right bank, we came to the extensive ruins of the palace of the Chinese king, whose power was overtaken by the father of the reigning monarch. Although this event took place only forty years before, the ruins might be supposed, from their appearance, to be centuries old.' These interesting buildings are unfortunately not normally open to the public.

3

The Major Temples

THERE are so many temples in Bangkok that one is embarrassed by the necessity of mentioning but a few. A great many, however, are relatively recent foundations by pious persons and without much historical or artistic interest. Crawfurd, one of the earliest outside observers of early Bangkok, could write:

I ought, however, to observe that the first appearance of a Siamese temple made a forcible impression upon us. It was impossible to see the exterior of the buildings, and the laboriousness and costliness of their workmanship and materials, without feeling that we were amongst a numerous people, who had made considerable advances in civilisation . . . .

However, not all observers were so generous: Sir John Bowring observed in the middle of the nineteenth century: 'At daybreak, went to see one of the large pagodas of Bangkok. They are ornamented in a barbaric style of gorgeousness; hideous figures of every sort are stuck around them.'

Here then is a personal selection of six, not including the magnificent Temple of the Emerald Buddha (Wat Phra Keo), already described in the pages relating to the Grand Palace.

Wat Phra Chetuphon (Wat Po)

In the previous chapter it was indicated that Wat Po existed prior to the founding of Bangkok. It dates, in fact, from the seventeenth century when it was known as Wat Potaram. It was enlarged by Rama I and the renovation took seven years, five months and twenty-eight days to complete, and the chronicles, which provide this information, noted in great detail all that was done. In 1801 a ceremony of dedication was held. It was this enlarged temple that Crawfurd visited in 1822 and left a long and detailed description of all that he saw. Rama III, in 1832, built the chapel containing the statue of the reclining or sleeping Buddha, which is what it is perhaps now most famous for. It is also a centre of traditional Thai medicine. In a pavilion in one of the courtyards are marble tablets describing the practice of Thai medicine, which were set up on the order of Rama III, who, in his restoration of the temple which began in 1832, desired to make the wat a kind of exhibition of all the knowledge of the time, an early university. Lastly, it is famous for the formerly much copied marble reliefs around the base of the bot telling the story of the Thai version of the *Ramayana*.

The temple is surrounded by a huge wall, and the main entrance in Tanon Chetuphon is in a road separating the temple buildings from the monks' residences. The sixteen gates are guarded on the inside by statues of giants. The main temple building leads from the entrance and is surrounded by a cloister with rows of gilded Buddhas in different styles and shrines in the middle of each wall. The bot is raised on a marble platform and at its base are the 152 marble bas-relief panels of the *Ramayana* scenes. Art students and others used to make a good living by copying these, putting rice paper on top of the originals and dabbing an ink-soaked stocking on the top; but the authorities have banned this practice for fear of ruining the originals. The inside of the building, which unfortunately is not often open to the general public, is very grand with its thick pillars, fresco-covered walls and bronze chandeliers, and the external doors are inlaid with fine designs in mother-of-pearl also showing scenes from the *Ramayana*. Several chedi surround the building and its cloister.

To the left of this group of buildings are four big chedi, built to house the ashes of the early Chakri kings (the fourth was added later), the pavilion dedicated to the study of Thai medicine, a library decorated with porcelain pieces in the shape of flowers, and gardens and miniature hills which decorate the temple compound. To the north-west is the large building constructed to shelter the reclining Buddha. The crowds of tourists are usually such that there is unfortunately little feeling of reverence and authenticity in the visit. The statue, made of brick covered with plaster and gilded, is some 45 metres long and 15 metres high and shows the Buddha entering nirvana; it appears squashed into the building around it and one can only see satisfactorily the mother-of-pearl inlaid feet showing the 108 auspicious signs by which the true Buddha could be identified. The swarms of tourists and attendant postcard, soft drink and souvenir sellers give a certain animation, though they are not normally associated with nirvana. Bowring, in 1856, described the statue thus:

The Great Buddha is about 140 feet in length. I imagine he must be built of brick, covered with chunan, and then with a thick leaf of gold. He lies in the ordinary state of repose, reclining on his left hand upon richly-decorated pillows. The soles of the feet are made of ebony, covered with mother-of-pearl symbols resembling those which are found in the various impressions which are deemed sacred....

Wat Suthat

This temple is much less visited than Wat Po, though in fact it is far more impressive. It was begun in 1807 by Rama I, decorated by his son and only completed in the reign of his grandson. It has two main buildings, the bot, surrounded by a cloister, on the side of the temple near the Giant Swing, and the huge vihara, at right angles to this.

The whole complex is dotted with a great number of stone Chinese statues, altars and decorative pieces, as well as bronze horses. The statuary is said to have been brought to Bangkok as ballast in ships which had carried rice to China. A lot of it is rather fanciful, showing Europeanized soldiers with hats and trousers, often unfortunately damaged now, but still not without charm (Colour Plate 4).

The bot has a high roof and three huge doorways with finely carved and gilded door panels, one of which is said to have been carved by Rama II (Colour Plate 5). Crawfurd, who, as was noted previously, was one of the earliest visitors to Bangkok from the West, could write in 1822 that it was still under construction, and mentions favourably the 'noble chamber' of the bot. The interior, which has columns, contains the enormous and most graceful statue, Phra Buddha Chakyamuni, brought down from Sukhothai by Rama I (Colour Plate 6). The statue is in the attitude of the Buddha subduing Mara and is made of bronze. It came from Wat Mahathat in Sukhothai and is one of the largest metal images of the Buddha in Thailand. The walls have fresco paintings showing the life of the Pacceka Buddha and in the corners are scenes of the *Ramakien*, the Thai *Ramayana*. The life of the historical Buddha is shown above the windows and, as usual, the conquest of the Buddha over the temptation of Mara faces the altar. The very long vihara is outside the cloister and is said to have been built between 1839 and 1843 and is less successful than the bot in its proportions. The paintings on the inside walls, which are being restored, are often of considerable interest. Unusually, there are no pillars. Like the bot, the interior of this building is often closed to the public.

Wat Rajabopit

This charming temple was built in 1869 on the orders of King Chulalongkorn and is found just outside the confines of old Bangkok between Klong Lord and the river. It has recently been splendidly restored (Colour Plate 7). The entrance doors are guarded by moustachioed soldiers carved on the wooden gate panels. It has a curious plan of a high gilded central chedi with the bot and the vihara to the right and the left, the three buildings linked by a circular cloister.

The doors of the sanctuary to the right are finely inlaid with mother-of-pearl showing the five royal orders and are set off against the porcelain tiled walls and gilded door entrances. The interiors of the two shrines are in Thai Gothic (Colour Plate 8). Inside the chedi is a Lopburi period Buddha (*c.* 700–1400) seated under a naga.

The wat, which was one of King Chulalongkorn's preferred temples, underwent many changes in the course of its existence, like most others. The original paintings which decorated the walls of the bot, in traditional Thai style, were covered up in 1929, and the walls remain plain today. It may have been this temple to which the American missionaries referred with qualified approval in a publication dated 1884:

Heretofore, preaching-halls have been bare within, but the present king has lately built a beautiful Gothic chapel, after the most approved modern style—stained glass windows, an altar, pews for the congregation, and something that has the appearance of a grand organ, with great pipes running to the ceiling, but, alas! a niche in each pipe filled with a small idol, and a much larger one on the altar. Still, the departure from old customs shows His Majesty's desire for improvement.

There are certainly no signs of pews or an organ today, however (nor are there in the only other Gothic temple in the country, at Bang Pa-In), though clearly the temple underwent major changes in 1929.

The temple is completed with numerous monks' dwellings and meeting-halls, many of which are handsome buildings, all in a relatively small space. On the canal side, opposite the main entrance from Tanon Tong Tanao by Ban Mo, is a collection of gothic chedi and stupa containing ashes of deceased notables and looking rather like a European cemetery of the nineteenth century.

Wat Borworniwes

The temple by the very active Banglampoo market is rather off the usual tourist paths but forms an extremely interesting ensemble of buildings. It was built by Rama III from 1824 to 1832 and it was here that Prince Mongkut, the future Rama IV, became abbot in 1832. He had entered the monkhood in 1824 when his claims to the throne had been passed over, and was abbot at Wat Mahathat before where he founded the new priestly order known as Thammayut. Here he studied Latin and English with the aid of missionaries who came to the country in the reign of his half-brother. The strict order which he founded is centred on this temple and it is not only the temple in which all subsequent kings have spent some time as an ordained monk, as tradition requires, but also the home of one of the few Buddhist universities in the country.

The growth in importance of this institution has somewhat detracted from the former charm of the compound, since new buildings have crowded onto once-empty courtyards and spaces. Nevertheless, the tortoise-filled shady canals that flow through the grounds past the elegant monks' quarters, including the residence of past royal monks, the Pra Tamnak Panya, a three-storey European-style residence built for Prince Mongkut by Rama III, are still attractive.

The main shrine faces Prasumane Road (in which there is a restored section and gateway of the old city wall). The entrance is decorated in porcelain and the building inside is T-shaped, with a Sukhothai Buddha statue, Phra Buddha Chinasara, on the main altar at the crossing. The building seems higher than it is inside because of the rows of square pillars on both sides.

The wall paintings are of particular interest, dating from the period of Rama IV and introducing, for the first time in Thai murals, a concept of perspective. On the lower levels, between the doors and the windows, are shown the daily activities of the monks (Colour Plate 9). The people on the columns are classified by type according to colour. The scenes above, showing horse-racing, a surgeon removing a cataract, ships sailing across the sea, and people contemplating a large lotus, all exemplify Buddhist teachings. The colours of the background are dark. Permanent Western-style houses in brick are shown, and the views were taken from early nineteenth-century prints. Krua In Khong, a painter-monk from Petchburi, was ordered by Rama IV to paint these scenes as an allegory of the Dharma. The groups of Western ladies and gentlemen walking across the grounds of imagined palaces are entirely unexpected.

Behind the main building is a gilded chedi of no great beauty and in the grounds are two Buddha statues from the Lopburi period, an early Javanese Buddha statue, a Dvaravati Buddha image and a Buddha's footprint. In one of the vihara at the back is a sleeping Buddha; both have wall paintings. One is decorated with scenes from the Romance of the Three Kingdoms (like the Chinese pavilion in Wat Po) and the other shows monkish pursuits.

Wat Benjamabopit

It cannot be said that this particular temple is off the tourist track. It is extremely popular with visitors because of the lavish attention to detail and the well laid-out and cared-for grounds which like Wat Borworniwes also have canals and bridges, but on a much grander scale.

It is not an old temple, having been built by King Chulalongkorn in 1899. As he had to pull down two small temples in the grounds of his new Dusit palace area, he had one large new temple built on the site of a nearby shrine. Prince Naris, a noted artist and half-brother to the king, was in charge of the construction.

The main temple building contains a copy, made in 1920, of

the famous Phra Buddha Chinarat statue in Pitsanuloke. The paintings in the bot are almost monochrome, like architectural drawings, and show important stupa and prang in the kingdom. The windows are filled with stained glass with yellow as the dominant colour. The cloister at the rear contains a collection of Buddha statues of all the periods in Thai history. Some are original and some copies. Behind the bot is a large bronze Lopburi Buddha in kingly attire which is much respected. Two stone Dvaravati Buddha statues are in niches in the southern wall of the cloister.

The Marble Temple, as it is popularly known, is a modern temple on a grand scale, built and maintained with taste in handsome grounds in a part of Bangkok which was very much Rama V's creation. The dwelling in which he lived as a monk in 1873, which was originally in the Grand Palace in Suan Sivalai, was reconstructed in the grounds of Wat Benjamabopit between 1900 and 1905 and contains contemporary exhibits. It has paintings showing the king's travels in Europe and Asia, theatrical scenes, and the reconstruction of the chedi of Nakorn Pathom.

Wat Arun

The Temple of the Dawn, as the temple is known in English, is not strictly speaking in Bangkok but in Thonburi. It faces the river and its high pointed shape in the form of a Khmer prang is a symbol of Bangkok.

The temple is an old one and was originally known as Wat Makok (probably the same 'kok' as in Bangkok). King Taksin, in whose time it was known as Wat Cheng, is said to have passed it at dawn and to have vowed to restore it. Taksin built his palace next to the temple buildings and the temple was attached to the palace, in the manner of the Temple of the Emerald Buddha. Taksin removed the monks who were originally

10. Grande pyramide en l'honneur de Buddha, à Bangkok, 300 pieds de haut (Pallegoix, 1854)

there. The Emerald Buddha was kept here until it was taken across the river to the building Rama I constructed to house it in his palace grounds.

Rama II, when crown prince, in 1785 undertook the restoration of Wat Arun, gave it its present name, and enlarged the size of the prang. This was not completed until the reign of Rama III but he died before the monument could be dedicated. The huge prang (Plate 10) is 81 metres high and the mass rests on piles driven into the soft river bank. There are four steep stairways, one on each side, leading to the three terraces, with smaller prang at the corners and pavilions at the base of the stairways. It is usually held to symbolize Mount Meru.

Apart from the silhouette, the decoration is remarkable. It is covered in bits of broken porcelain. Close to, this simply looks odd, but from a distance it achieves its full effect of colour, design and glitter. Young is correct to note (1898): 'Thousands upon thousands of pieces of cheap china must have been smashed to bits in order to furnish sufficient material to decorate this curious structure. It must be admitted that though the material is tawdry, the effect is indescribably wonderful.'

The other structures in the temple are less remarkable; most were restored in the reign of Rama IV. The bot has a cloister around it and is reached through a huge doorway, guarded by protective porcelain-covered giants. There are double rows of columns and frescoes on the inside, dating from the fifth reign. The outside has impressive porticos at each end. There is a small square mondop between the bot and the vihara, which is less elaborate than the bot and has some gilt statues inside.

Seen from the river, as it is meant to be viewed, the temple is undoubtedly impressive, more particularly at dusk (in spite of its name), with the sun behind it. Seidenfaden, in his 1928 *Guide to Bangkok*, allowed himself a lavish description on the subject:

...at sunset when the fiery ball of the king of the day disappears behind the tall leafy trees which form a frame around the towers and temple buildings, then the five prang stand out against a scarlet background, a background which slowly changes its colour to rosy tints and then to mauve, until finally the black shadows of the night envelop the whole fabric. Indeed a more wonderful or impressive picture than this can hardly be imagined.

One might not put it in such colourful prose, but the Thai decorative genius, putting to effective use pieces of broken porcelain in a striking setting, is nowhere better illustrated except possibly in the compound of the Temple of the Emerald Buddha.

4

The Growth of Bangkok

BANGKOK started, as we have seen, as a city of floating houses (Plate 11), which every early traveller described as being the most remarkable thing about the place. Only the Grand Palace and the temples were initially on terra firma. Gradually, as the power of the dynasty was consolidated, and as the royal family expanded, the princely houses and the dwellings of the nobles, then of richer citizens and others, also moved on to land. Finlayson, who accompanied Crawfurd on the 1821–2 mission to Siam, could write:

The city is continuous with the palace, extending on both sides of the river to the distance of three or four miles; it lies principally on the left bank.... The town is built entirely of wood, the palaces of the king, the temples and the houses of a few chiefs being alone constructed of brick or mud walls....

The few streets that Bangkok boasts are passable on foot only in dry weather: the principal shops, however, and the most valuable merchandise are found along the river in the floating houses. These floating houses are occupied almost exclusively by Chinese.

There was in Bangkok a British merchant, Mr Robert Hunter, 'a gentleman for many years resident in Siam, and who had the esteem and regard of all the better portion of the inhabitants of Bangkok, his Majesty the King included' (as Earl wrote in 1837); he lived in the city from 1824 to 1844 and initially was successful and influential, even being granted a title by the king in 1831. He was, however, to lose this influence because, in direct violation of a royal edict, he imported opium and also because when the Siamese traded themselves, as the king and his nobles increasingly did, he had powerful com-

11. Floating house on the Menam (Bowring, 1857)

petition. Earl hoped Hunter would write up his memoirs after a residence of several years in the country, but he did not do so. According to Neale, writing in 1852, it was Hunter who obtained permission from the crown for foreigners to reside on houses built on land. Nevertheless, even during his time, Bangkok still on first impression appeared largely a floating city:

...the whole city of Bangkok, consisting of a long double, and in some parts treble, row of neatly and tastefully-painted wooden cabins, floating on thick bamboo rafts and linked to each other in parcels of six or seven houses by chains...rose like a magic picture to our admiring gaze.

An earlier visitor to Bangkok, Malcom (1838), admittedly a somewhat prejudiced missionary, juxtaposed the splendour of the temples with the other buildings of the capital:

One cannot avoid contrasting the size and costliness of the sacred edifices with the meanness of the city in other respects. The houses are small and rude, and the streets in general nothing more than footpaths, overgrown with bushes, bamboos and palms. Every species of filth and offal is thrown among these bushes; and the state of the air may be supposed. Every few rods, a canal or ditch is to be crossed; and a log, or plank or two, without a handrail, is generally the only bridge; those of the principal thoroughfares are better, but none are good or neat. Of the numerous canals, not one is walled up or planked, except sometimes to secure a Wat. Most of them are left bare at half-tide, presenting a loathsome slime, and filling the air with stench, besides being useless half the time. Not an effort seems to be made by the authorities to improve the city.

The floating houses, which so much struck early visitors, were to remain a feature of the riverscape at least until the end of the nineteenth century (Smyth still remarks on them in 1898).

The area around Klong Lord was the first to be developed, but Bangkok spread and the second canal ring of Klong Banglampoo followed in 1785, to be fortified afterwards. The third canal ring of Klong Padung Krung Kasem was built in 1851–4. The Thiphakorawong Chronicle noted for 1861:

In the third month the foreign consuls all signed their names to a petition which they presented to the King [Rama IV]. It said that the Europeans were used to going out in the open air, riding carriages or riding horseback for pleasure. These activities had been good for their health and they had thus not suffered from illnesses. Since their coming to live in Bangkok, they had found that there were no roads to go riding in carriages or on horseback for pleasure and they had all been sick very often.

The king agreed to this request and by his death in 1868, New Road (Charoen Krung) extended south of the city and there were several roads within it. The chronicles record this but noted, 'However, there were no bridges. Assistance which would result in merits for the donors was solicited from

12. Inside the city wall (Hesse-Wartegg, 1899)

noblemen and wealthy Chinese men to build bridges over the canals where the newly constructed roads crossed them.'

One road, however, does not make for radical change; Mouhot in 1864 wrote, 'Bangkok is the Venice of the East and whether bent on business or pleasure you must go by water'.

Royal rides were made to visit the developing city; the press on 2 December 1870 noted: 'H.M. the King and a retinue of princes drove out on the Krung Charoen Street. There was also a large retinue of several hundred horsemen. The Royal drives will be of great benefit to the streets of the city as it necessitates cleanliness and the repairs of both streets and bridges' (quoted by Smith). However, not all were over-impressed; Bock, writing in 1884, said: 'The main road, or Krung Charoen, which is several miles in length, is itself often partly under water during the south-west monsoon and the back lanes and bypaths which constitute the principal means of communication are in a chronic state of filth, wet or dry.'

In the reign of King Chulalongkorn, sections of the city wall (Plates 12 and 13) were demolished to provide foundations for

13. The city wall (Carter, 1904)

roads (Plate 14); so also were the fortifications of the Wang Na, the palace of the second king, which occupied part of the Pramane Ground. It was said that 200 kilometres of carriage-ways were built, with elegant bridges of iron or marble over canals, some of which still survive.

As had been noted in the previous reign, bridges were essential for roads in a city crossed by numerous canals. A survey carried out in 1887 reported a total of sixty-seven bridges, of which twenty-two were wooden and twenty-four apparently in need of repair. A number of foreign engineers, mostly Italian, were employed by the Department of Public Works on designing elegant bridges. King Chulalongkorn in 1894 gave a sum of money equal to the number of days of his age multiplied by a quarter of a baht (one *salerng*) to build bridges, and seventeen bridges, called Chalerm Bridges, were built for each succeeding year of his reign, including two completed after his death.

Perhaps the most beautiful of all was the Makawan Rungsun Bridge over Klong Padung Krung Kasem on Rajadmanern

14. A street in Bangkok (Carter, 1904)

Avenue, a steel structure with concrete slabs, well-proportioned pillars, curved marble bases and elaborate wrought iron railings.

The bridge was over the principal thoroughfare constructed in Rama V's time: Rajadamnern Avenue (the 'royal way for walking') linked the Grand Palace with the new palace area in the suburbs of Dusit. This street was lined with palaces and used less for walking than for riding on horseback or more often in carriages and, at the end of the century, for the royal craze of cycling. At the beginning of this century it was also the scene of processions of motor cars, the itinerary of which was carefully announced in the newspapers, and the novel sight preserved for posterity in early photographs (Plate 15).

Bangkok early on acquired the distinct communities which had so struck the early travellers to Ayutthaya and whose territorial locations were clearly marked in all the Dutch and French maps of the former capital in the seventeenth century. The Portuguese community settled around the Santa Cruz church on the Thonburi side, the Chinese were of course at Sampeng right from the beginning and as a community

15. Motor car celebration along Rajadamnern in 1908. Motorcades were popular in the later years of King Chulalongkorn's reign.

continued to expand in size and wealth throughout the nineteenth century, though being assimilated by intermarriage as few Chinese woman came as immigrants. Gutzlaff, writing in 1833, remarked that all the races which came to Siam were absorbed by it and lost their distinctive characteristics: '[the Malays] generally lose, as almost every nation does in Siam, their national character, become industrious, conform to Siamese customs, and often gain a little property.' He found this particularly deplorable with respect of the citizens of the Celestial Empire, whom he was anxious to convert:

[the Chinese] even throw away their jackets and trowsers [sic], and become Siamese in their very dress...if they have children, these frequently cut off their queues, and become for a certain time Siamese priests. Within two or three generations, all the distinguishing marks of the Chinese character dwindle entirely away; and a nation which adheres so obstinately to its national customs becomes wholly changed to Siamese.

16. Tramway in Bangkok. The city had one of the earliest systems of electric tramways.

This apparent absorption was only partly true, since the different communities remained clearly distinct until the process of assimilation took place. There was and still is a Vietnamese quarter in Samsen known as Ban Yuan, a Malay quarter, and an Indian (sometimes called Kling by early visitors) community in Phahurat. The Makassarese had their district at Makassan. The Mons, the Khmer and the Lao, with their distinctive dress and hair-styles, were easy to identify (it was only in the reign of King Vachiravudh, for example, that the long skirt or *pasin* of the Lao was adopted as a model dress for ladies who until then, like the men, had worn the *panung*, the cloth which was drawn between the legs and tucked in the waist at the rear).

A 1928 guide to the city advocated taking trams (Plate 16) for local colour (the author makes no mention of omnibuses, presumably below the dignity of European visitors, and which Young in 1898 described as long shallow boxes on four wheels, without springs and with a rickety roof, crowded and packed). On the electric trams, Seidenfaden wrote:

... will be found sitting together yellow-robed Siamese monks, long-bearded Arabs, sarong-clad Malays, voluble Chinese who would appear to keep no secrets from the outside world and yet keep many, dark-skinned Tamils, Burmese, Mon, the panung-clad Thai and members of a host of other races.

Early writers not only remarked on the distinctiveness of these different races, but went to great lengths to try to enumerate them, ending up with wildly contradictory figures. As foreign consuls with extraterritorial rights established themselves from the middle of the nineteenth century, this question of numbers became important, particularly as the colonial powers, notably France and Britain, increasingly claimed jurisdiction over so many peoples in countries near Siam.

Crawfurd, in his *Descriptive Dictionary* of 1856, said:

The present reputed population of Bangkok is 404,000, composed of the following nationalities, namely, Siamese, 120,000; Laos, 25,000; Malays, 15,000; Peguans, 12,000; Burmese, 3,000; Portuguese Christians, 4,000; and Chinese of the whole, or mixed-blood, 200,000.

There is no doubt but that Bangkok is a populous and busy place, but the probability is, that the estimate of the number of its inhabitants is greatly in excess.

These figures in fact were taken unchanged from Pallegoix (1854), who himself said that the figures were 'd'après les ambassadeurs anglais et américains qui l'ont visitée plusieurs fois', therefore including Crawfurd himself. Mouhot (1864) noted that 'it is impossible to state the exact population of Bangkok, the census of all Eastern countries being extremely imperfect', but remarked that it was estimated as being between 300,000 and 400,000.

As the city expanded, so did the number of temples increase. Those built in the reign of Rama III were strongly influenced by Chinese decorative tastes and this continued into the reign of Mongkut. A good example is Wat Thepthidaram on Mahachai Road by the outer city wall, where the basic structural shapes are Thai but the surface decoration, such as the stucco gables with ceramic pieces, is almost entirely Chinese. This temple was built by Rama III for his daughter Princess Apsorn Sudathep, and curiously it was here that Thailand's most famous poet, Sunthorn Poo, in disfavour under Rama III, lived as a monk from 1840 to 1842.

The Golden Mount in the grounds of Wat Saket (Plate 17) was begun in this period but Rama III abandoned the project when the structure started to give way. Rama IV took up the challenge and completed the hill, placing a chedi and an enclosed gallery around it on the top (these however were not completed until the next reign). It was designed like its forebear at Ayutthaya as an artificial hill, the replica on earth of Mount Meru, to be a focal point of observation for the city. Until the 1960s it was still one of the highest points in Bangkok and commanded an extensive view of the river and what still seemed like a profusion of trees and gardens. The temple at the base became the location of an important annual fair in November, but one tends to forget that it had a less carefree past. Bock in 1884 spoke of it as a 'terrible sight', and Sommerville, writing in 1897, described it as 'one of the most offensive and horrible sights of Bangkok', because it was used as a cremation ground for the poor and destitute of the city. He spoke of the ashes of human remains, dogs gnawing bones, the vultures gathered on the 'silk-cotton-trees' and dead prisoners being tipped out of the boxes on which they were brought in: 'One of the custodians quickly raised the body of the prisoner up in the box and with a sharp knife cut a number of strips of flesh from the arms and thighs and callously threw piece after

17. Wat Saket and canals, an early view of the city

piece to the more greedy birds, who eagerly crowded around . . . .' There was a proposal to establish guns on the top of the hill when the French were blockading the river in 1893, but the king turned down the proposal, perhaps mindful of the damage the guns might do to the city (one hundred years later, in the coup attempt of 1985, shells aimed from tanks at a radio antenna nearby landed on the other side of the river many kilometres away from their target). The hill remained defended: '. . . since the time of the Franco-Siamese trouble it is guarded by soldiers, and no one is allowed to pass the sentries on duty without a permit . . .' (Young, 1898).

Although always recognized as far more wholesome than Batavia, Bangkok was not without its squalor and health problems. Everything was tipped into the canals, and King Mongkut's order requiring people to desist from putting dead animals in the waterways had as little effect in his time as today. Cholera first came in 1819, from India, and the following year many people died. The almanac of the time recorded: 'On the 7th month, the waxing moon, a little past 9 o'clock in the evening, a shining light was seen on the north-west and multitudes of people purged, vomited and died.'

Epidemics came in 1849, 1868, 1873 (when 6,660 were noted to have died), in 1880 and until the early twentieth century. During cholera epidemics, Bock wrote, up to 120 bodies a day would be brought to Wat Saket and laid before the vultures. The palace had its own water supply brought from the hills of Petchburi. Christian medical missionaries introduced vaccination against smallpox in 1840 but Smith records: 'When I went to Siam in 1902 some 8 to 10 per cent of all the people that one met in the streets were scarred by the disease. Twenty years later it was a rare sight.'

All early visitors remarked on the extreme personal cleanliness of the Siamese, probably a good deal better than their European counterparts (this was certainly so in the seventeenth century).

Consolidation could be found for privations of 'civilized' amenities by the expatriates in various ways. Ladies when sitting outside wrapped themselves in big brown paper bags drawn up around their skirts to prevent attacks of mosquitoes; gentlemen found excuses for indulging in alcohol: 'A certain amount of alcohol is more necessary for one than it is in England. It helps out the less nourishing food, and turns the mind from trivial worries,· which are often unduly magnified by the heat and mosquitoes of tropical life' wrote Lieutenant-Colonel Forty in

1929. Food was of course different, but sometimes too much so. Neale, in 1852, seems entirely prejudiced:

Of all Oriental cookery, however, the Siamese is the most execrable and unwholesome; not from the want of the wherewithal to cook (for most certainly the pork and poultry were remarkably fine), but from want of *savoir faire*, and from the abominable practice they have of eating pickled garlic, and flavouring all their dishes strongly with this unsavoury condiment.

Certainly the ships bringing Western food were eagerly awaited by expatriates, as can be seen from the announcements in the newspapers of the time when they arrived. It was not just the Westerners who imported foodstuff of their choice. Before ice factories became common, wealthy Thai families as a great treat would buy ice imported from Singapore and use it with their desserts and drinks on grand occasions (Plate 18). Most learned to adapt; in the words of Forty:

... hustle and worry are utterly out of place in a hot country. Orientals as a body refuse to bustle, and cannot understand why we should. Once the European realises that there is nothing at all worth worrying about, and that even if there were it would not be of the slightest use, all will be well with him.

Fatalism and the belief in one's karma meant that all accepted what happened with little attempt to struggle against destiny. This was not always very kind. A fairly genial form of slavery still existed untouched until 1873, the selling of children was common (and is not unknown today), corvée labour existed until 1905, debt bondage was the rule. Bowring remarked upon the number of people one saw going around the city in chains, and Neale could write in 1852:

The public prisons are like so many bird-cages suspended over the water; here debtors, like so many sparrows, keep hopping from one

18. Child with top-knot and champagne glass. This is almost certainly a
modified celebration of the traditional top-knot cutting ceremony.

19. King Chulalongkorn leaving Bangkok Noi station, Thonburi, for his southern tour. The King promoted the construction of railways as part of the effort to modernize the country.

side to the other, as the shade shifts, and they are dependent upon the charity of passers-by for what they get to eat and drink. Women of notorious ill-fame are also similarly confined, with this difference, that their cages are on the rafts next to the banks of the river, so as to be hidden from the public gaze.

and even as late as 1884 Bock noted:

Passing along the main road one seldom fails to hear the clang! clang! of heavy chains dragging along the ground. Presently the sound is explained by a gang of prisoners passing by, chained together two and two, with a heavy iron collar round the neck of each, from which hangs an iron chain connecting them together: heavy rings are also round the ankles, with chains again connecting the two feet of each prisoner.

However, King Chulalongkorn's reforms and desire for improvement had their practical benefits too. Electricity came and lit the main streets, and in 1894 electrified tramways were introduced (Plate 16), earlier than in many European cities. By 1900 there were 17 kilometres of lines. The Bangkok Water

Works was constructed in 1914. Railway construction started earlier, in 1891, and the first line was the Paknam railway, a private line (the tracks of which can still be found in parts) which ended at what was to be the new Hua Lampong railway station, though the southern line, not completed until the early twentieth century, ended at Bangkok Noi in Thonburi (Plate 19) until the Rama VI bridge was built. In 1883 a postal service was started and the postal roll gave the population as approximately 169,300, of whom Thais numbered 136,000 and Westerners 300. This is at considerable variance with Crawfurd's population statistics (which he himself called into doubt) of half a century earlier. The postal service (Plate 20) drew much praise in its early days; Smyth could note in 1898: 'Of all Siamese officials the postman, with his neat jacket and his native *panung*, whether in the capital or the jungle, is the smartest, the most polite, and I need hardly say, the most welcome.'

Given its marshy soil and the absence of real physical limitations, Bangkok rapidly spread outwards since it could not go upwards. King Chulalongkorn, after his return from Europe in 1897, started a spate of development, particularly in the newly laid out Dusit area. Maps of the period anticipate this development (Plate 21, a map of the 1890s, shows Dusit as already existing which is not, in fact, the case). Seidenfaden in 1928 could speak of 'a city of great distances' and recommended the hiring of carriages to take one from the five hotels of the time (Phya Thai Palace, the former home of Rama VI, the Oriental by the river, the Royal in Sathorn, the Europe in New Road and the Rajadani at Hua Lampong station) to places as far away as the Throne Hall at the end of Rajadamnern Avenue, the Grand Palace and Wat Po.

The post-war explosion, particularly from the mid-1960s, would leave the earlier travellers breathless, not only for the dimensions but also for the pollution which the ubiquitous

20. Postman, 1892

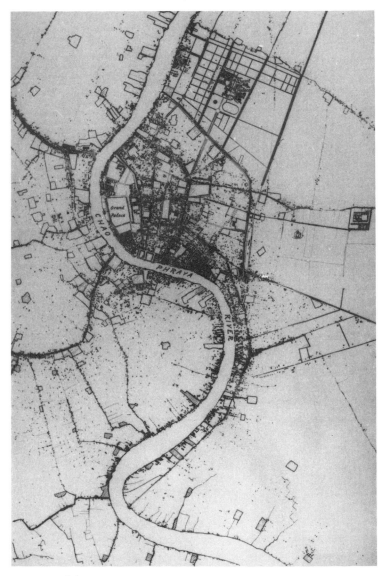

21. Map of the 1890s

motor car has introduced. The water-borne garden city grew rapidly and as it grew it changed its nature; the built-up area in 1900 covered 13 square kilometres and in 1981 330 square kilometres, by when most of the old canals had been filled in and the city was prone to serious flooding. Somehow the city services kept pace, though only just. The normal daily functioning of Bangkok is something of an astonishing miracle. But some things, both good and bad, have not changed. The *Bangkok Times* of 1929 complained that the telephone service in Bangkok was 'the worst in Asia'. But the geniality of the Thais, on which all early travellers remark (with the exception of Earl), remains fortunately untouched.

Phra Buddha Yod Fa Bridge (the Memorial Bridge), the first across the river, was opened on 6 April 1932, 150 years after the founding of the city, an answer to an old prophecy that the dynasty would last only 150 years. King Prajadipok was hoping at the same time to present his people with a constitution, but his plans were thwarted by senior princes in the Supreme Council. The coup of June 1932 overthrew the absolute monarchy and established a constitutional role for the throne, though no one could pretend that the constitutional path with its numerous coups, counter-coups, constitutions drawn up and abandoned, has been painless. The celebration of the bicentenary on the foundation of Bangkok, in 1982, was done on a suitably lavish scale, and the wholesale restoration of major monuments which was undertaken was both a considerable achievement and a justifiable manifestation of national pride.

5
Traditional Survivals

THOUGH modern Bangkok seems to have thrown away its ancient watery charms in preference for development on the model of Los Angeles, with which its name as well as its physical aspect is obliquely associated, there are, fortunately, numerous survivals of its more gracious and relaxed past. The palaces and the old temples most obviously recall the origins of the city as a royal creation with royally endowed places of worship. But there are also numerous other remnants of the old Bangkok which are there to be discovered by the curious.

After the palaces and the temples, there are key canals (Plate 22) which remain and which have not been filled in during the rush to modernize in the 1960s. The original canal, Klong Lord, constructed to make the Grand Palace and associated buildings an island, remains. Starting by the new Phra Pin Klao Bridge, the path of the canal passes under the road by what used to be the Royal Mint, completed in 1902, but what is now the National Art Gallery. It then goes by the back of the Ministry of Justice, the Ministry of Defence, the Ministry of Foreign Affairs, the tiny Wat Rajapradit, founded in 1864 and built on a foundation of old water jars, with its fine mural paintings of the time of King Mongkut showing scenes of daily life (Colour Plate 10) and its excellent pediments, and the statue of the pig erected in 1913 in honour of Queen Saovapha by three senior persons born in the same cyclical year (she was born in 1893, the year of the pig, and it was an object of importance to her). Opposite is the gracious exterior of the Ministry of the Interior (Colour Plate 11), and the canal then goes past the cemetery of Wat Rajabopit to the area of Ban Mo, the old goldsmiths' quarter, and the vegetable market of Pak Klong Talart. A walk along the

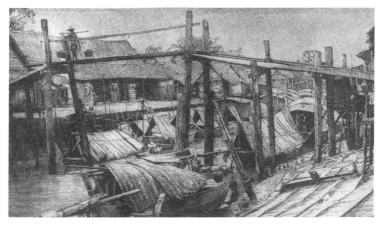

22. Canal view (Hesse-Wartegg, 1899)

banks of this canal is a walk through the earliest part of Bangkok.

The second canal, Klong Banglampoo, starts by the restored fort at the bend in Phra Artit Road, goes past the old market of Banglampoo; in which until quite recently there was a functioning *likay* or folk opera theatre, under the Saphan Fa Bridge where Rajadamnern does a dog's leg bend, past the Golden Mount and the grounds of Wat Saket (Plate 17), through the Chinese market quarter of Sampeng and the Indian cloth quarter of Phahurat to end rather ingloriously in a muddled area below the Memorial Bridge.

The third ring canal also remains, though like Klong Banglampoo is much less well preserved than Klong Lord. Klong Padung Krung Kasem starts by the flower market of Talat Thewet and Wat Thewarat Kunchon on the upper reaches of the river, goes past Wat Makut and Wat Somanat and the United Nations building by the gracious bridge supporting Rajadamnern Avenue, Makawan Rungsun, and then follows a southwards direction of a strictly commercial nature, going past the railway sidings behind which is hidden the temple of Wat Boromniwat with its paintings by Krua In Khong who also did those at Wat Borworniwes, besides Hua Lampong station, under Rama IV Road and into the river after passing the congestion of New Road.

Virtually nothing remains of the four parallel canals by Siphaya, Suriwong, Silom and Sathorn Roads except the unlovely concrete embankments of Sathorn Road. Two major east–west canals survive though, running from the river to the former eastern marshlands which were peopled in the reign of Rama I with Muslim prisoners from a southern campaign. These are Klong Samsen, starting by the river above Krung Ton Bridge near Samsen Road and following a rather undistinguished course north of the Victory Monument, through Dindeng to Bangkapi, and a little to the south, and Klong Saenseap, branching from Klong Padung Krung Kasem and running at the back of Petchburi Road. At the few points where these two canals are visible from the roads, it can be readily seen that they have ceased to be effective waterways, clogged as they are with refuse and slime.

It is in Thonburi that the canals remain in daily use as waterways, bathing places, washing areas, and streets. The huge loop, following an old bend in the Chao Phraya River, of Klong Bangkok Noi, Klong Chak Phra, Klong Bangkunsi and Klong Bangkok Yai, remains a major artery for long-tail boats, vendors and in parts tourists, though those taken on the southern extension of Klong Bangkok Yai to Klong Dao Kanong are now more likely to see their fellows than natives. The Thonburi floating market has effectively ceased to exist. Having said this, it does not mean that selling and buying along the canals in Thonburi has stopped; far from it, simply that the early morning collection of market women in their boats selling fruit, meat and vegetables at a particular point is one of the things of the past.

The temples of the Thonburi side, some of them pre-dating the foundation of Bangkok, are singularly rewarding. They remain for the most part in relatively unspoilt surroundings and many have mural paintings of exceptional charm, though some of these are in a sad state of preservation. Wat Kalayanimit is found on the river by the beginning of Klong Bangkok Yai and dates from Rama III; it is one of five new temples built by the king in his reign. As might be expected, there are numerous signs of Chinese artistic influence in the decoration of the temple courtyard. The paintings inside the bot are traditionally Thai, however. To the left of the bot is an exceptionally high vihara and the grounds contain many Chinese statues, said to have been brought originally as ballast, as with Wat Suthat. A little further along the canal is Wat Hong Rattanaram; it is an old temple restored in Taksin's reign. It has exceptionally good carved doors and pediments, a handsome Sukhothai Buddha statue and a fine library in its grounds.

Wat Raja Orot, off Bangkok Yai on Klong Dan, is a shady nineteenth-century temple started by Rama II and completed by Rama III in the Chinese style. It has been held to be a folly of Rama III. It presents a group of buildings of considerable interest; the paintings in the bot are still very good, being still lifes in the Chinese style, and no people are shown. The mother-of-pearl doors have Chinese-style dragons on them and are among the best in Thailand.

Wat Chaiya Thit is best reached from Klong Bangkok Noi. Though it is not easy to find, it is well worth the search, for in spite of its unprepossessing exterior, the bot contains some of the best mural paintings in Thonburi, dating from the early Bangkok period and in very good condition.

Near the beginning of Klong Bangkok Noi is the most impressive of all the Thonburi temples as far as mural paintings is concerned, and this is Wat Suwannaram. The bot and the vihara face the canal; though the temple dates from the

Ayutthaya period, the buildings are from the early Bangkok period, and were restored by Rama III, being completed about 1831. The paintings inside the bot are said to have been executed by Kru Thong Yu (Luang Vichit Chetsada) and Kru Khongpae, who was of Chinese descent, both well-known painters of the period. Between the windows are scenes from the ten last *Jataka* tales, being the stories of the previous lives of the Buddha. The tenth, the *Vessantara*, is always more elaborately treated, and starts on the lower level of the wall behind the altar and continues all along one side between the windows. At the level above these are four superimposed rows of persons in prayer turning towards the altar. The wall on the inside of the doors shows, as is common in the layout of these paintings, the victory of the Buddha over the temptations of Mara, and on the rear wall behind the altar is the Buddha coming down from heaven, with representations of the three worlds, heaven, earth and hell.

Of interest in all these paintings is the false perspective, or rather lack of it, that allows different scenes to be shown at the same time on a single panel. The strange hair-style prevalent in the time of Rama III is clearly seen: 'Both men and women have their hair shaved from their heads, with the exception of a small round patch which is left between the crown and the forehead. This being brushed up, is made to stand on end, which gives them a scared appearance' (Earl, 1837). Usually, somewhere in the paintings, which are true to local conditions and contemporary life-styles, one can also see the all-important betel box and its accessories.

Nearer to the river, still on the Thonburi side, are a number of interesting temples. A little to the north of Wat Arun is Wat Rakang, a building of considerable historical importance. The main temple building is an elaborate and gracious structure with fine stucco work on the outside and curious tempora paintings dating from the reign of Rama VI which show scenes of the Grand Palace and other buildings of old Bangkok (Colour Plate

1. Modern oil painting of Rama I, in the library, Wat Rakang, Thonburi.

2. The Grand Palace seen from the river. This illustration appeared in colour on the front of *Le Petit Journal*, Paris, 12 August 1893.

3. The octagon, Vimanmek Palace, reconstructed in 1901.

4. Chinese ballast statue of a Western soldier.

5. Side door of bot, Wat Suthat, *c.* 1810.

6. Painting by Nai Won: The arrival at Ta Phra of the Sukhothai Buddha statue destined for Wat Suthat, in the Varophatphiman Hall, Bang Pa-in, c. 1880, reproduced by gracious permission of His Majesty King Bhumiphol of Thailand.

7. Inner courtyard and doorway, Wat Rajabopit, 1869.

8. Interior of bot in Gothic style (the original paintings have been removed), Wat Rajabopit, 1869.

9. Detail of a painting by Krua In-khong: A monk's ordination in Bangkok, a scene from contemporary life in the city, in the bot of Wat Borworniwes, c. 1855.

10. Mural of Loy Krathong festival in Bangkok, from Wat Rajapradit, c. 1864.

11. Ministry of the Interior, by Klong Lord, a typical European-style building of the late nineteenth century.

12. Mural showing an imaginary attack on the Grand Palace, in the vihara of Wat Rakang, Thonburi, 1922.

13. Front of library, Wat Rakang, Thonburi, the home of Rama I before he became king.

14. Mural showing a royal barge, in the vihara of Wat Rakang, Thonburi, c. 1922.

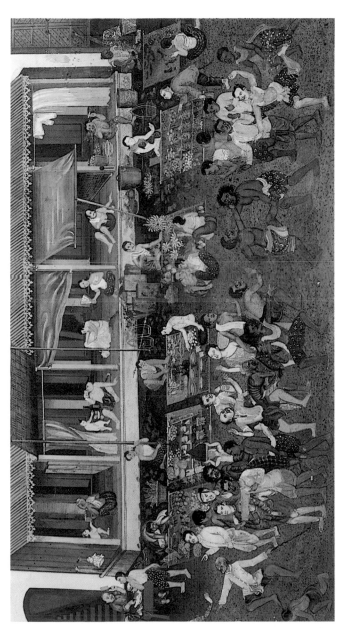

15. Seesuwan goes to the market, a scene from Phra Aphai Manee, in the Varophatphiman Hall, Bang Pa-in, c. 1900, reproduced by gracious permission of His Majesty King Bhumiphol of Thailand.

16. The Kamthieng House, The Siam Society, an old northern house from the nineteenth century re-erected in Bangkok in 1966.

12). They were painted between 1922 and 1923 by Phra Wanawatwichit (Thong Charuwichit). The importance of the temple is in its magnificently restored library, or Ho Trai (Colour Plate 13). It is a classical Thai wooden building in three parallel sections, with some original paintings by Phra Acharn Nak on the inside and fine carved eave supports on the outside which are known as *kan toey*. The building was once used as a temporary residence by the founder of the Chakri dynasty before he became king. It was he who ordered the removal of the building to its present site to be used as a library about 1788 and he also commissioned the paintings. They are rich in details of contemporary life. The building also has two excellent old bookcases, and the original doors, now inside and replaced by copies on the exterior, are masterpieces of their genre. There is also a fine carved pediment over the door.

To the north of the mouth of Klong Bangkok Noi, a little away from the river, is the small temple of Wat Dusitaram, which was reconstructed in the reign of Rama I and changed many times afterwards. It has extremely fine paintings inside the bot, probably dating from the reign of Rama III, which are equal in quality to those at Wat Suwannaram and show a similar disposition. The three worlds are shown on the rear wall, in great detail, but between the windows and doors are episodes from the life of the Buddha. There are three levels of praying devotees. Above the windows are some interesting carved picture frames.

Continuing north on the Thonburi side of the river and a little away from it, past the Phra Pin Klao Bridge, is Wat Bangyikan, with fine porticoes and more wall paintings of good quality, though they are not in good condition.

Another temple worthy of note on this side is Wat Thepnimitr, which in spite of its somewhat run-down appearance, has again good mural paintings in a building that seems to date from Rama I. It virtually forms part of another temple,

Wat Phakininat, which has a good pediment on the vihara and some paintings left inside.

Temples and canals are not all that there is to see of interest in Thonburi to remind one of the old Bangkok. The Royal Barges are housed in a building just inside Klong Bangkok Noi. These were used in solemn procession when the king went to present robes to the monks, usually at Wat Arun at the end of the rainy season and the Buddhist lent (Colour Plate 14). The barges by themselves constituted a sight for visitors as early as 1822, when Crawfurd was taken to see them. The barges are long and narrow, elaborately carved and gilded. The oldest dates from the reign of Rama I and is one of the finest, with its prow in the shape of a swan's neck which gives the vessel its name, Si Suwannahong, and its stern in the shape of a naga. A platform in the middle of the boat has a pavilion for the throne. The boat is rowed in unison by fifty oarsmen while a singer chants poetic texts. The barges are very difficult to manoeuvre on account of their size and height above the water. There are several other barges of note dating from different reigns and a full procession can consist of some thirty-five vessels. The procession in the early days of Bangkok was an annual feature, but it has only been revived occasionally in recent times. The Dynastic Chronicle of the First Reign records that a new barge was built and:

... on one occasion the King ordered a grand Kathin Robe Donation Procession. The robes to be presented to monks from the court were taken on the *Ekkachai* Barge in procession. Members of the royal family, nobles, and government officials were all asked to construct boats for the royal procession according to their ability and imagination. Some were done in the shape of a crocodile, some in the shape of a shell, some in the shape of a fish, or other sea animals. Musical instruments were also in these boats. The procession went around the capital city, and the King himself went to present the monks robes according to the custom. It was a grand occasion.

One can be sure it was.

Thonburi still has vestiges of its fruit orchards, as it was in the time of King Narai. Crawfurd noted in 1822 that 'the culture of fruit trees seems to be the most advantageous that can be followed so near the capital. Among these orchards here and there occur a temple'. It seems strange that a few metres from the roads can still be found oases of peace where rambutans, coconuts, durians, jackfruit, mangoes and mangosteens are grown on raised dikes with parallel water canals between to provide drainage in the otherwise marshy soil. The orchards have shrunk considerably in size as the city has expanded, but small family fruit-tree plots remain.

Not far from Wat Rakang on the Thonburi side, at the back of Siriraj Hospital, are located a number of foundries for casting Buddha statues. The craft has hardly changed in technique with the centuries. The moulds are designed and prepared for pouring by workmen, the bronze is poured in and left to harden for one or two days, and the joints in large statues are smoothed over using a hammer, chisel and sandpaper (in the past this last was not used, but the leaves of the koi tree, a plant of the Urticaceae family). The same foundries also produce large temple bells and sometimes statues of particularly revered monks.

Boat building is still carried on in various parts of Thonburi near the main canals and also by the river. Only rarely constructed now in the Bangkok area are the huge rice barges, laden to the gunwales and so low in the water that the river seems about to fill them, but the long-tailed boats, used for daily transportation in Thonburi by people who work in Bangkok and come to the Ta Phra and Ta Chang landings on the Bangkok side, are still commonly constructed. They are now all fitted with outboard motors which are sawn-down versions of lorry engines and just as noisy; they gain in speed what they lose in charm.

Musical instrument makers can be found scattered over the city in a few isolated establishments. This is a family craft; one family is found near Rajadamnern Avenue, at the back of the Board of Investment. The instruments of the Thai traditional *piphat* orchestra, notably the percussive *renak-ek* (xylophone), the *klong* (drum) and the *kong wong yai* (circular set of gong kettles), the stringed instruments of the *saw-oo* (alto fiddle), the *saw-duang* (two-stringed fiddle) and the *chakey* (zither), and the *klui* or flute, require expertise and long training to produce. Bock, a century ago, noted that the Siamese greatly prized their instruments and he was unable to buy a complete set; only an occasional item was available in a pawnshop. They command very high prices, if the quality is good, and of course the demand is fairly limited, particularly since the younger generation has taken with great readiness to guitars of both the natural and electric varieties.

Silk weaving was a craft traditional in the north-east and continues to exist only on an industrial scale now in Bangkok. Virtually all Bangkok looms have now been automated.

Perhaps the most exotic of the traditional crafts still plied are the gold beaters, no longer found in Tanon Tee Tong (Gold Beaters' Road), as one would expect from the name, but across Rajadamnern Avenue, behind the Suksaphan Store. There a row of muscular young men pound at small slabs with special hammers. The base of the pad is made of buffalo hide and pieces of pure gold no thicker than a sheet of paper and exactly 1 square centimetre in size are placed between transparent copying paper and built up like a sandwich, some 400 to 500 pieces on top of each other. Another piece of buffalo hide is placed on top. The pile is beaten with some 300 blows on each side, not in the same position, and then turned over for similar treatment. As the gold gets warm with the beating, it spreads; the rhythmic pounding must not stop or the gold will get cold. Finally each piece becomes about 10 centimetres across and it is then cut into four of five pieces and sold to the faithful in the temples for applying to Buddha statues and thereby gaining merit for the giver. Both gold beating and Buddha statue making tend to be family occupations, passed from one generation to another.

Chinatown, starting in Sampeng and now extending all the way down New Road, remains as traditional as ever. It is virtually impossible to drive down this section, and certainly impossible to see much if one does. It is far better to walk down a part of the road and see the teeming activity of the shop-houses, the narrow lanes covered with awnings of rags to protect passers-by, the food stalls selling a variety of more or less appetizing comestibles, and the small Chinese temples devoted to an amalgam of Confucianism, Taoism, and Buddhism, wreathed in the smoke of incense and burning paper. A number of traditional Chinese crafts continue to be practised here, including the making of paper lanterns and the altars considered necessary by every self-respecting shopkeeper of Chinese descent. Bock, in 1884, gave a description still almost true today: 'On all sides are Chinese joss-houses, Chinese carpenters' shops, Chinese cabinet works, Chinese carriage manufactories; wherever there is work going on it is sure to be under the sign of a Chinese proprietor.'

One thing that has changed is that the illegal opium houses, which were still a feature of the quarter in the early 1960s, have disappeared. But Chinatown is not for the delicate; Smyth dismissed Sampeng in 1898 as 'Chinese Bangkok, malodorous and ill-mannered'.

Lastly, one should perhaps mention the traditional entertainments. The theatre has always figured large in the Siamese horizon, and the courts of both Ayutthaya and Bangkok were usually extremely fond of theatrical performances. There still exist a number of charming photographs of King Chulalongkorn's court in fancy dress and performing in plays or dance-dramas; his son Rama VI was passionately interested in the theatre, writing plays, producing them and acting in them.

The court dances of *khon* and *lakorn* are, as one would expect, stately and slow and involve much subtle movement of the fingers, wrists, arms, and feet, but relatively little of the rest of the body. The actual tales are largely derived from the *Ramayana* epic and the Story of Inao, assembled from Javanese sources by Rama II, a great patron of dance, drama, music and verse, unlike his successor who discontinued support of the theatre and accidentally encouraged its popularity by the dispersal of the royal troupes. Thai classical dancing is not liked by every visitor; like all entertainments that originated in the courts, it is slow and mannered. Kukrit's court-raised heroine saw in a performance exquisite refinement that overcame age:

The most eagerly awaited event—an episode from the dance-drama *Inao* performed by the famous dancers of the Palace—also took place in Sivalai Garden. It was a Royal private affair and Ploi considered herself blessed by good fortune to be among Sadech's retinue and therefore a member of the audience. The dancers were the Chao Chom and the Chao Chom Mothers under the previous reign—under King Mongkut; they had retired from the stage many years ago, had become living legends, and Ploi had been hearing about their incomparable artistry ever since she had been in the Inner Court. That night had her spellbound . . . .

This contrasts with the opinion of Young, expressed in 1898, who obviously had little time for the art: 'The ladies go through a series of posturing evolutions euphemistically called dances. They are nothing more than extraordinary contortions of the body accompanied by equally strange motions of the limbs.' Performances now take place irregularly at the National Theatre and at the universities.

Likay, the popular folk opera, with its impossible plots and still more impossible costumes, used to be a feature of every temple fair, and can still be found performed in parts of the city

23. *Likay* dancers. This traditional entertainment, in the form of folk opera, was very popular in the nineteenth century.

(Plate 23). It is bawdy and vulgar and thoroughly enjoyable, providing one understands a little of what is meant to be going on. There is now no permanent *likay* theatre, however.

The *ramrong* dance, moving slowly round one's partner without ever touching, again is a feature of all temple fairs, though these days one has to pay a few baht for the privilege of dancing with one of the girls lined up along the wall for the purpose. A whistle starts and stops the dance according to the clock rather than the music.

Gambling technically is banned, but card-playing and card-throwing are widely practised in secret, and cock-fights are not unknown in the city. Many Thais, like the Chinese, have traditionally had a strong inclination to gambling. Bock noted in 1884:

All the gambling houses I have seen in Bangkok are of the commonest description: large bamboo sheds, with an atap roof, devoid of furniture, and many of them without even a floor, only the bare earth, over which are laid mats for the players to sit on. Over every mat, or at least over every gambling party, stands a book-keeper, who watches over the interests of his master, the proprietor of the den.

Establishments of this kind have probably passed into history however. Today, less sordid settings are found for playing Thai chess, *makrut*, which is played everywhere at all times of the day and night, and in times of high unemployment is a great distractor, like betting on Siamese fighting fish which are widely raised in jars and put to fight.

Bangkok, which to the uninitiated visitor, may seem to have lost all its traditional occupations and activities, in fact still continues to possess corners and crafts much as it must have done in the time of Rama I.

6

Oases in the New Bangkok

THE transformation of Bangkok to an American-style city of electric poles, billboards and cars has fortunately not been complete and just as there are traditional survivals into the late twentieth century, so too there are oases of calm still to be found here and there.

Bangkok is, for a city of its size, rather lacking in open spaces, but there are effectively five parks which, on Sundays and public holidays, tend to be very crowded. The Pramane Ground (Sanam Luang) by the Grand Palace is an open space rather than a park, and until fairly recently was the scene of a lively weekend market. It still remains a focal point of the city, especially on major holidays like New Year's Eve or the King's Birthday, when the old tamarind trees around the grass core are illuminated with thousands of coloured lights.

The Sanam Luang is still the scene of the ploughing ceremony, when the omens of the future harvest are foretold by court Brahmins according to the grain selected by the buffaloes harnessed to the plough, and remains the location of all major royal cremations, such as that for the late Queen Rampai Barni in 1985. The dull ochre building to the west of the grounds, now part of the National Cultural Council and formerly the National Library, was in fact built as a permanent *meru* or pyre for cremations, but its use was changed in 1917 since it was considered that giving permanency on earth to the spirits of the dead might not be a good thing. Next to it is Wat Mahathat, built in the reign of Rama I by the second king. The main buildings were all destroyed by fire in 1801 and now consist of a mondop and two symmetrical buildings, the bot and the vihara with some fine wooden carved pediments. This temple was the place where a religious council was held to revise the Siamese tripitaka in 1788 and where Prince Mongkut was abbot before going to Wat Borowniwes. It is now the seat of the Buddhist University founded by King Chulalongkorn in 1889 for the Mahanikaya sect. Buddha amulets are sold here and also a kind of truncated weekend market operates on Saturdays and Sundays.

Sanam Luang is also the scene of popular kite-flying contests in the hot season from March to May, when teams of players pitch the huge male *chula* kite against the more wily long-tailed female or *pakpao* kite.

The small Saranrom Gardens by the Ministry of Foreign Affairs, though not properly a public park, are what remain of the gardens laid out by Rama IV and turned by Rama V into a zoo before Dusit was opened. Wat Rajathiwat is in one corner and for years the gardens were the site of an important annual fair. They contain a Chinese pagoda and some other decorative structures.

A part of the Dusit Palace area, adjacent to the Throne Hall, has become a zoo, and this again is extremely popular on weekends, especially, as might be imagined, with children. Most of the white elephants presented to the monarch are now kept here and treated much less lavishly (and a good deal more healthily for their own good) than in the past. They are elephants which, in fact, are usually grey but distinguished from their brethren by special signs or characteristics and which fascinated early travellers to Thailand. The days have gone when they were considered a god-like manifestation on earth, though they are still treated with considerable respect. The Dusit Zoo also has a good collection of monkeys, bears and other animals, birds and reptiles, though a better collection of snakes is to be found at the Red Cross Institute, the Sathan Saowapha, on Rama IV Road, where the venom of snakes is extracted for use as antidotes to snake bites.

Lumpini Park was created by King Vachiravudh and intended to be the site of a grand national exhibition, which came to nothing with his death. His statue, a scene of nocturnal assignations, is at the junction of Silom and Rama IV Roads. The park, originally considered 'vast', has been reduced in size and value by the construction of too many kiosks and restaurants.

There is one newly created park, Chatuchat, to the north of the city near the Laadprao intersection. This is quite extensive and when built was considered too far out of the city; as the city has spread, of course, it has become something of a centre in its own right, particularly since the weekend market moved here from the Sanam Luang. Though the weekend market can hardly be referred to as an oasis, it is certainly a very traditional market, and extremely popular. Everything is sold: pets, clothes, food, antiques new and old, flowers, plants, furniture, anything you could desire, or almost. A number of stalls are run by authentic hill tribespeople selling traditional embroideries as well as contemporary clothes in their own fashion; this is a considerable change of recent times, for twenty years ago one almost never saw hill tribespeople in the capital.

The many temples of Bangkok nearly all have, in some degree, courtyards which provide a respite from the noise and dust of the city streets and some are architecturally of interest. One popular with visitors is Wat Traimitr, in the Chinese quarter by Chaeroen Krung or New Road. The temple buildings are of little interest, but the famous Golden Buddha is found here. It is from the Sukhothai period, is 3 metres high and is a good example of statues of the period. Its gold content was discovered by accident in quite recent times, for its was originally covered in plaster. It was dropped when being moved to a new site and some of the stucco fell off, showing glimpses of gold beneath. It was probably covered with plaster during one of the Burmese invasions of Ayutthaya as a protection against it being looted, and was brought down, covered in stucco, to decorate a temple in Bangkok after the foundation of the new capital.

Two curiosities survive in the old city from its early past. One dates from the foundation of the city, being the Lak Muang, or foundation pillar. This used to be obscured by a petrol station right opposite the Grand Palace, but this has fortunately been removed and the new shrine of the foundation pillar erected on the site. The Dynastic Chronicle records that the Lak Muang was erected before the palace and at a precise astrologically-determined time: '...the ceremony of raising the zero milestone of the new capital city was performed on Sunday, the tenth day of the waxing moon of the sixth month at 6:54 in the morning.' The pillar is made of wood and lacquered and gilded; it is reputed to bring good luck and fertility to childless couples. It is endowed with a great number of legends relating to its construction. People offer flowers and pray before the pillar, and classical dances are performed near by. Outside crickets can usually be found in cages waiting to be released by those who wish, for a small sum, to gain merit. A similar shrine which has accumulated much merit and many garlands is to be found in a corner of the Erewan Hotel at the busy intersection on Ploenchit and Rajdamri Roads. This, however, is completely modern and in the form of the god Indra. It is interesting to observe motor-cyclists abandoning their handlebars to make a gesture of respect to this statue as they pass at full speed.

The other survival in the old city is the Giant Swing, Sao Ching Cha (Cover Plate; Plate 24), in front of Wat Suthat. It consists of two enormous slightly inclining teak posts joined by a carved cross-beam at the top and was used for an annual festival in honour of the Brahmin god Siva. Teams of young men swung on a boat-like structure suspended from the cross-beam and tried to snatch a bag of money tied to the top of a

24. Giant Swing in action. The ceremony was discontinued in the reign of Rama VII.

specially-erected post near by. The ceremony has not been held since the reign of Rama VII and the swing itself, repaired in 1920, is a replacement of the original (paid for by the local company founded by the son of Anna Leonowens, the English governess of King Chulalongkorn).

Near by is an old Brahmin temple, which Crawfurd mentions being taken to see in 1822, and which contained some interesting statues now in the National Museum. The temple is small and architecturally undistinguished, but remains the centre of Brahmin devotees; Brahmin priests still serve, as has been seen, at certain court functions and are a curious survival in a Buddhist court. They originally came to Ayutthaya from Angkor after the Thai conquest of the Khmer capital, and the Ayutthayan kings, seeking to take over the mantle of the Khmer empire and legitimize their claims to power, took over these rites as well. The modern City Hall, of remarkable ugliness, is opposite the Giant Swing, though to the east of Wat Suthat is a shady square leading into a labyrinth of lanes in a Chinese quarter. All around are some of the early commercial streets of old Bangkok; some of the old shops survive, with modest stucco pediments above their windows and occasionally elegant decoration (Colour Plate 15). Vincent noted in 1873:

Near this part of the city the late King has laid out several streets at right angles to each other, and built upon them compact blocks of two-storey brick houses, which are now rented by the Government . . . to the people. The present King has followed the example of his royal father in these civic improvements . . . [and] is also accustomed to take the air in a barouche drawn by six horses with liveried postillions . . . .

Three private homes are open to the public and between them provide a glimpse of often gracious living of a bygone era. Suan Pakkard Palace in Sri Ayutthaya Road, is the home of Princess Chumpot of Nagara Svarga. The buildings by the street consist of five traditional Thai wooden houses which are decorated with old Thai furniture, drums, porcelain and so on. The Khmer and early Mon statues are remarkable. There is a particularly fine collection of Ban Chieng pottery, among the earliest known anywhere, along with beads and other decorative items found on the site in north-east Thailand. Set in the beautiful gardens of the palace is the famous Lacquer Pavilion which Prince Chumpot found serving as a disused library in a temple near Ayutthaya. The building is raised on piles and consists of two distinct buildings, a Ho Trai or library and a Ho Khien or writing room. The panels are of black lacquer with gilded designs of carefully observed details of daily life, nature and the animal world. Some people in Western costume of the seventeenth century are also shown, but such decorative motifs are not unknown in later Thai Temples; the appearance of such persons does not mean that the library dates from the seventeenth century. Boisselier considers that the style is similar to that found in the paintings at Wat Rakang and the Buddhaisawan chapel, and dates the building from the reign of Rama I. One of the attractions of Suan Pakkard Palace is that it is a real home, still inhabited by the Princess (who, however, mostly lives in a modern air-conditioned building), who has been for many years an important patron of the arts.

Another private home, no longer inhabited though by its owner, is Jim Thompson's house, located near the National Stadium (another building of remarkable ugliness) in Soi Kasemsarn 2, and facing on to a rather smelly part of Klong Saensep. Thompson revived the Thai silk industry after the Second World War and built his own home from a number of traditional Thai houses which he had brought down to Bangkok and assembled on this site. There used, in fact, to be traditional silk weaving taking place along the canal near by. The house contains an excellent collection of stone carvings, Buddha heads and traditional Thai paintings. Thompson disappeared in mysterious circumstances in the jungles of Malaya and his house and collection remain in Thailand. Although the house is not in itself old, all its components are, and like Suan Pakkard it is a private home, built as such, decorated with taste and housing a valuable collection of Thai antiques.

The other traditional home which can be visited is not, in fact, typical of the Bangkok region, but comes from the north near Chiengmai. This is the Kamthieng House (Colour Plate 16) in the grounds of the Siam Society in Soi Asoke (Sukhumwit Soi 21). The Society is a learned body dating from 1904, and in 1963 it acquired as a gift this northern house, which was dismantled in 1964 and erected on its present site in 1966. It has been attractively arranged as a traditional village house, complete with cooking utensils and appropriate decorative items, rice barn, wagons and carts, and to which has been added a fine collection of old wood carving coming mostly from northern temples. Although never a house in the old Bangkok period, it is a typical country house and is well worth visiting.

As one might expect, there are a number of extremely gracious private homes with fine collections of antiques, but these are not open to the public. They are scattered all over the city, in no particular area. Some are reconstructed from old Thai wooden houses in the central plains, some are original buildings from the early Bangkok period. Glimpses can be had of them by accident as one passes down the street or soi, sheltering behind thick foliage of large shady gardens.

Some of the more public early embassy buildings have survived, particularly those by the river, where the French and Portuguese Embassies remain in early nineteenth-century buildings of considerable charm, though perhaps some inconvenience to their occupants. The American and British Embassies occupy large compounds but are relatively new structures. Of the 'cosy cottages' Seidenfaden talked about as existing in 1928 on Sathorn Road, few remain, though the appropriately rose-coloured Soviet Embassy is in a surviving period building.

Most of the old streets with canals on either side and huge shady rain trees above have gone in the name of modernization. With a great deal of imagination one can picture how Wireless Road looked twenty-five years ago, for many of its trees remain, and the parallel side roads were once klongs. It is impossible now to conjure up a similar picture of Ploenchit, though less than thirty years ago it was the same.

Perhaps, and appropriately, only the streets on the east, south and west sides of Chitralada Palace remain unscathed, with their canals on both sides of the carriageway and big shady trees above. Long may these remain.

Epilogue

THE collapse of Ayutthaya in 1767 after a long drawn-out siege and a period of decline was not, with the benefit of hindsight, to be entirely unexpected. The rapid pulling together of the country under Taksin was remarkable but his choice of Thonburi for his capital, the old Bancok, already the site of two forts, was less surprising. Rama I, fearing the continuing power of the Burmese armies and mindful of the exposed position of Thonburi, moved his capital across the river in 1782 and he himself is said to have announced his dynasty would last 150 years. Certainly its untrammelled power lasted this span, but the dynasty survives and provides stability in a region beset with problems.

The first three kings of Bangkok recreated their capital on the model of the fallen Ayutthaya, though Rama III's reign was marked by strong Chinese artistic influences. With Rama IV, and particularly after the signing of the Bowring treaty and similar agreements with other powers, Siam no longer looked to the past and inwards, but outwards to the world; the capital began to reflect this. Rama V's long reign, not without external and internal political difficulties, saw a continuing expansion and marked modernization of the capital, and though it remained a garden city of canals, it took its first steps towards elegance and city planning.

The early twentieth century saw this trend continue in the royal palaces and public buildings, but the concrete blight of the 1930s, which affected so many capital cities in the world, was less kind to Bangkok than most. The rapid expansion of the capital from the 1960s completely changed the appearance of the capital, and not for the better.

An attempt has been made in these pages to show that it is only the surface of this city face that has been changed. A little wrinkled, perhaps a little tawdry at times, Bangkok has its elegance and its charms if one knows where to look for them. These are for the most part not in the foreign ghettoes of Sukhumwit Road or the sprawling suburbs to the north, but in the old heart of the city, by its river and in the former Bancok of Thonburi.

There is a general movement of nostalgia for the past at the present time and Kukrit Pramoj's novel, *Four Reigns*, and its success is one manifestation of this. Another is the conscious effort now being made to preserve the memorials of the past, and though modernization is inevitable and certain to continue, it is to be hoped that it does not have to be of the senseless and destructive kind which has in recent times characterized much of that which has taken place in Bangkok as elsewhere. The lavish restoration of old monuments in 1982 for the celebration of the foundation of the city 200 years before is a sign of the pride now being taken in the city's past.

This does not mean that all is perfect, of course. There have been many suggestions to abandon the capital entirely and start again somewhere else. Such counsels of despair are not surprising, but are for a number of reasons, not least cost, vested interest and tradition, unlikely to be heeded. Bangkok, warts and all, looks like remaining the Thai capital. The City of Angels is threatened by developers, floods, pollution, uncontrolled motor traffic and uncontrollable immigration. But more than any other capital in South-East Asia, it remains a vibrant city. Its numerous relics of the past, described in this short book, contribute in no small degree to its poise and its refinement.

Appendix

List of Bangkok Kings and Ranks

Kings

Reign	Name	
1767–1782	Taksin	(King of Thonburi)
1782–1809	Rama I	Phra Phutthayotfa[a] (Phraya Chakri)
1809–1824	Rama II	Phra Phutthalaetla Naphalai: son of Rama I
1824–1851	Rama III	Phra Nangklao: son of Rama II
1851–1868	Rama IV	Mongkut: son of Rama II
1868–1910	Rama V	Chulalongkorn: son of Rama IV
1910–1925	Rama VI	Vachiravudh: son of Rama V
1925–1935	Rama VII	Prajadipok (abdicated): son of Rama V
1935–1946	Rama VIII	Anand Mahidol: grandson of Rama V
1946–	Rama IX	Bumipol Adulyet: grandson of Rama V

[a] Kings had different names before assuming the throne, during their reign, and after their demise. Rama I reigned, for example, as King Ramathipodi, and Phra Phutthayotfa was a posthumous title.

Ranks

Inherited (Royal)[b]

1st generation (for child of a major queen)	Chao Fa	(Royal Highness)
(for child of a lesser wife)	Phra Ong Chao	(Highness)
2nd generation	Mom Chao	(Serene Highness)
3rd generation	Mom Rachawong	(no equivalent)
4th generation	Mom Luang	(no equivalent)
5th generation	(commoner status)	

Conferred (Commoner)[c]

1st rank	Chao Phraya
2nd rank	Phraya
3rd rank	Phra
4th rank	Luang
5th rank	Khun

[b] This is not complete and not invariable; princes and princesses could be raised in rank by the monarch. *Chao Chom* is a title confined to royal concubines.

[c] An additional title was given to each individual in addition to the general rank title, and this individual title would change each time a person was granted a higher title.

An exceptionally high rank of *Somdet Chao Phraya* was sometimes conferred.

Since 1932 only the female titles of *Tanpuying* and *Khunying* have been conferred.

Glossary

Bot (*ubosot*). Preaching and ordination hall in a temple.

Chedi. Tapering spire normally containing relics and standing on its own.

Ho trai. Library in a temple.

Kan touey. Carved eave supports.

Kinaree. A mythical bird in female form.

Klong. Canal.

Krung t(h)ep. City of angels, the official Thai name for Bangkok.

Mondop. Square library.

Menam. River.

Naga. Protecting snake of the earth or the Buddha.

Phom. Fort.

Prang. Khmer-style square spire.

Sanam luang. Royal ground (the Pramane Ground).

Soi. Lane (not originally a through road).

Stupa. Bell-shaped spire.

Tanon. Street.

Vihara (*viharn*). Large building in a temple where sacred objects are housed.

Wang. Palace.

Wat. Temple.

Bibliography

Batson, A. B., *The End of the Absolute Monarchy in Siam*, Singapore, Oxford University Press, 1984.

Beek, S. van, *Bangkok Only Yesterday*, Hong Kong, Hong Kong Publishing, 1982.

Birdwood, Sir G., ed., *Prince E. Ookhtomsky: Travels in the East of Nicholas II Emperor of Russia when Cesarewitch 1890–91*, Westminster, 1896, 1900.

Bock, C., *Temples and Elephants*, London, 1884, reprinted Singapore, Oxford University Press, 1986.

Boisselier, J., *La Peinture en Thailande*, Fribourg, Office du Livre, 1976.

Bowring, Sir J., *The Kingdom and People of Siam*, London, 1857, reprinted Kuala Lumpur, Oxford University Press, 1969.

Broman, B. M., *Old Houses of Bangkok*, Bangkok, Siam Society, 1984.

Campbell, J. G. D., *Siam in the Twentieth Century*, London, 1904.

Carter, A. C., *The Kingdom of Siam*, New York, 1904.

Clarac, A. and Smithies, M., *Discovering Thailand*, Bangkok, Siam Publications, 1971.

Crawfurd, J., *Journal of an Embassy from the Governor-General of India to the Courts of Siam and Cochin-China*, 2nd ed., London, 1828, reprinted Kuala Lumpur, Oxford University Press, 1967.

———, *A Descriptive Dictionary of the Indian Islands and Adjacent Countries*, London, 1856, reprinted Kuala Lumpur, Oxford University Press, 1971.

Dhaninivat, Prince, *The Royal Palaces*, Bangkok, Fine Arts Department, 1971.

Earl, G. W., *The Eastern Seas, or Voyages and Adventures in the Indian Archipelago in 1832–33–34, comprising a tour of the Island of Java, Visits to Borneo, The Malay Peninsula, Siam, etc*, London, 1837, reprinted Kuala Lumpur, Oxford University Press, 1971.

Fine Arts Department (Krom Silapakorn), *Wat Samkan Krung Ratanakosin* (in Thai), Bangkok, Fine Arts Department, 1982.

Fine Arts Department (Division of Archaeology), *The Sights of Ratanakosin*, Bangkok, Fine Arts Department, 1982.

Finlayson, G., *The Mission to Siam and Hué the Capital of Cochin China, in the Years 1821–22*, London, 1826.

Flood, T. and C., *The Dynastic Chronicles, Bangkok Era, First Reign*, Tokyo, Centre for East Asian Cultural Studies, 1978.

———, *The Dynastic Chronicles, Bangkok Era, Fourth Reign*, Tokyo, Centre for East Asian Cultural Studies, 1965.

Forty, C. H., *Bangkok: Its Life and Sport*, London, 1929.

Gutzlaff, C., *Journal of Three Voyages along the Coast of China in 1831, 1832, and 1833, with notices of Siam, Corea, and the Loo-Choo Islands*, London, 1834.

Hesse-Wartegg, E. von, *Siam. Das Reich des weissen Elefanten*, Leipzig, 1899.

Kukrit Pramoj, M. R. W., translated by Tulachandra, *Si Phaendin* (Four Reigns), Bangkok, Duang Komol, 1981.

Leonowens, A. H., *The English Governess at the Siamese Court*, London, 1870.

Loubère, S. de la, *A New Historical Relation of the Kingdom of Siam*, London, 1693, reprinted Kuala Lumpur, Oxford University Press, 1969, Singapore, Oxford University Press, 1986.

Malcom, H., *Travels in South-Eastern Asia, embracing Hindustan, Malaya, Siam, and China; with notices of Numerous Missionary Stations, and a full account of The Burman Empire*, Boston, 1838.

Moor, J. H., *Notices of the Indian Archipelago, and Adjacent Countries; Being a Collection of Papers Relating to Borneo, Celebes, Bali, Java, Sumatra, Nias, The Philippine Islands, Sulus, Siam, Cochin China, Malayan Peninsula etc*, Singapore, 1837.

Mouhot, H., *Travels in the Central Parts of Indo-China (Siam), Cambodia, and Laos. During the years 1858, 1859, and 1860*, London, 1864.

Neale, F. A., *Narrative of a Residence in Siam*, London, 1852.

Nengnoi Suksri, M. R.W., ed., *Palaces and Royal Residences in Bangkok* (in Thai), Bangkok, Chulalongkorn University Press, 1984.

Pallegoix, Mgr. J-B., *Description du Royaume Thai ou Siam*, Paris, 1854.

Presbyterian Board of Publication, *Siam and Laos, as seen by our American missionaries*, Philadelphia, 1884.

Prime Minister's Office, *Prachum Samut Parb Samkan nai Prawatsart* (in Thai), Bangkok, Prime Minister's Office, 1977.

Roberts, E., *Embassy to the Eastern Courts of Cochin-China, Siam, and Muscat; in the U.S. Sloop-of-War Peacock. During the Years 1832-3-4*, New York, 1837.

Seidenfaden, E., *Guide to Bangkok*, Bangkok, 1928, reprinted Singapore, Oxford University Press, 1984.

Sirichai Narumit, *Old Bridges of Bangkok*, Bangkok, Siam Society, 1977.

Sommerville, M., *Siam on the Meinam from the Gulf to Ayuthia*, London, 1897.

Smith, M., *A Physician at the Court of Siam*, London, Country Life, 1957, reprinted Kuala Lumpur, Oxford University Press, 1982, Singapore, Oxford University Press, 1986.

Smyth, H. W., *Five Years in Siam*, New York, 1898.

Sombat Plainoi, ed., *Nung Roi Roi-adeep* (in Thai), Bangkok, Studio 10, 1984.

Sternstein, L., *Portrait of Bangkok*, Bangkok, Bangkok Municipality, 1982.

Tomlin, J., *Journal of a Nine Months' Residence in Siam*, London, 1831.

Vella, W. F., *Siam under Rama III*, New York, Augustin, 1957.

Vincent, F., *The Land of the White Elephant*, London, 1873.

Wenk, K., *The Restoration of Thailand Under Rama I, 1782-1809*, Tucson, University of Arizona Press, 1968.

Wyatt, D., *Thailand: A Short History*, New Haven, Yale University Press, 1984.

Young, J. R., *The Kingdom of the Yellow Robe*, London, 1898, reprinted Kuala Lumpur, Oxford University Press, 1982, Singapore, Oxford University Press, 1986.

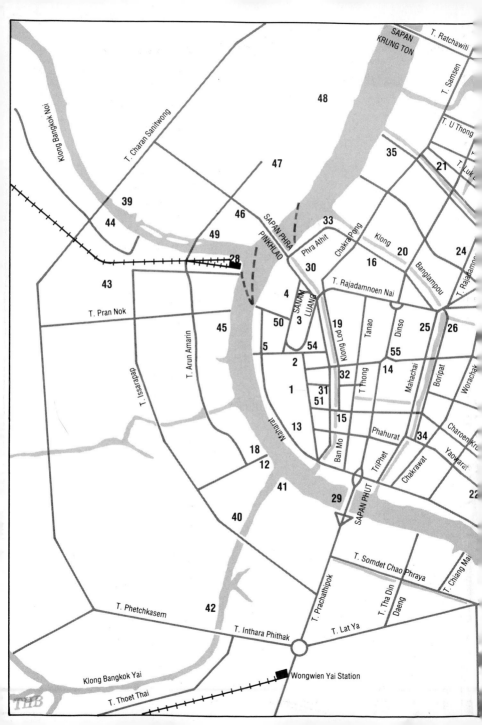